Embracing Cyprus

Embracing Cyprus

The Path to Unity in the New Europe

Pauline Green *with* Ray Collins

I.B. TAURIS

LONDON · NEW YORK

Published in 2003 by I.B.Tauris & Co Ltd
6 Salem Road, London W2 4BU
175 Fifth Avenue, New York NY 10010
www.ibtauris.com

In the United States and Canada distributed by Palgrave Macmillan,
a division of St. Martin's Press
175 Fifth Avenue, New York NY 10010

ISBN 1 86064 840 1

A full CIP record for this book is available from the British Library

Typeset in Stone by Dexter Haven Associates, London
Printed and bound in Great Britain by MPG Books, Bodmin

for the people of Cyprus
and
in memory of our friend and comrade
Yannos Kranidiotis

Contents

Foreword

Rt Hon. Robin Cook MP

Leader of the House of Commons
(Secretary of State, Foreign and
Commonwealth Affairs 1997–2001)

The division of the island of Cyprus is one of the remaining in-
justices of the Cold War era. It is not only a tragedy for its
people, both Greek and Turkish Cypriots, but it is an ever-present
reminder of the fragility of peace in the region. Overshadowed
for nearly three decades by the magnitude of the Middle East
conflict, it remains a major obstacle to better relations between
Turkey and Greece.

In the last decade, the only real window of opportunity for
a just and lasting solution to the Cyprus problem has been that
provided by the moves to bring the Republic of Cyprus into the
European Union.

There were some in the European Union who were reluctant
to contemplate Cyprus becoming a Member State unless the partition of the island was first resolved. We would all welcome the
restoration of Cyprus as a single united island, but if we made that
a pre-condition of admitting Cyprus to the European Union we
would run the risk of giving Ankara a veto. I always insisted that
the application by the Republic of Cyprus for full membership
should be treated on its own merits, which are stronger than
those of any of the other candidate countries. I'm proud that
Britain's voice was instrumental in getting agreement to the
decision at Helsinki that re-unification of Cyprus was desirable,
but was not an essential condition for its membership of the
European Union.

The irony is that the residents in the occupied north of the island would benefit most from membership of the European Union. Under the economic isolation imposed upon them by Denktash, their incomes have stagnated and are now well behind the level of the rest of the island. The prospect of the Republic of Cyprus becoming a member of the European Union offers a real incentive to people in the north to press their leaders for the division of the island to be removed in order that they too can benefit.

I have made many warm friends throughout the Cypriot community in Britain. North London contains a Cypriot community almost as large as half the population on Cyprus. I sometimes teased my good friend the Cypriot Foreign Minister that many of my Labour colleagues represented more Cypriot voters than his MPs in Nicosia.

Pauline Green was a good example. For a decade she played a leading role in the continuing work to keep the issue of Cyprus at the top of the international agenda. From 1994 to 1999, as the Leader of the European Parliament's largest political group, she worked assiduously to generate political space and opportunity for progress to be made in the search for a solution. With 120,000 Cypriots in her north London European constituency she was very conscious of the anguish of those who had lost family, homes and increasingly hope as the years went by without progress. In this work, she was aided and supported by Ray Collins, who became a regular contributor to the debate on Cyprus at international meetings across Europe. This book is a revealing insight to the motivations, quiet diplomacy and single-minded advocacy of their work.

Embracing Cyprus will become an essential tool for understanding the political and diplomatic issues surrounding the island and should be read by all who are interested in the workings of the European Union.

London
December 2002

Preface

A personal memorandum
Pauline Green

The island of Cyprus is truly captivating. Warm and friendly with beautiful natural contrasts, from the inviting blue Mediterranean Sea to cool beers in shady hilltop villages. The ideal place for a holiday, summer or winter. For most visitors this is the indelible image that they retain of their stay on this small island country in the eastern Mediterranean, whether they visit the large tourist centres of Limassol, Paphos or Aya Napa in the south, or the unspoilt port of Kyrenia on the northern coast.

That is unless they happen to turn the wrong corner in the island's sun-baked capital of Nicosia and walk into the barbed wire, the sandbags and the armed soldiers. Or unless they happen to take one of the many boat trips and turn their binoculars on the ghost town of Famagusta, once the most successful and thriving of Cyprus's tourist centres, its hotels and restaurants now empty and decaying, as they have been for the last three decades. Or unless they see the hills overlooking Nicosia adorned with the huge Turkish and Turkish Cypriot flags painted onto the hillside, or the blue flag of the UN fluttering from the many UN posts that straddle the so-called buffer zone that keeps the two Cypriot communities – Greek Cypriot and Turkish Cypriot – firmly apart.

For most visitors to Cyprus who do encounter the physical confrontation with conflict, there is a profound sense of shock. How? Why? When will it end? The dissonance between the beauty of the island and the warmth and friendliness of its people, both

Turkish Cypriots and Greek Cypriots with the stark image of fully armed soldiers maintaining the ceasefire line, with all the paraphernalia of war, cannot be underestimated.

The Cyprus problem was brought home to me in real terms when I stood for election for north London to the European Parliament in June 1989. Across the three London boroughs which I represented for the following 11 years lived some 120,000 Cypriots both Greek and Turkish. To very many of my Greek Cypriot constituents the Cyprus problem was a matter of the unwarranted invasion and occupation by Turkey in 1974 of over a third of the island, which had cost many Greek Cypriot lives, with over 1600 missing and 200,000 refugees denied the right to return, or even visit their family villages and their hurriedly abandoned property. To Turkish Cypriot constituents it was the legitimate intervention of Turkey in defence of the minority Turkish Cypriot community that since 1964 had felt itself forced into enclaves after Greek-Cypriot-inspired violence against their villages and extrajudicial summary executions often blamed on Greek Cypriot auxiliary police. No-one active in the politics of north London could survive without a detailed knowledge of the Cyprus problem, of its continuing impact on the lives of so many who live in London, let alone those who live on Cyprus itself.

The decision by the Government of the Republic of Cyprus to make an application for membership of the EU in July 1990 offered me a real opportunity to contribute to the efforts which would subsequently be made in Brussels to break the stalemate on a solution to the Cyprus problem.

The following pages lay out the strategy I developed to this end together with my long-standing political adviser Ray Collins during my early months in the European Parliament. This book is the story of our attempt to see that strategy through to completion. I have tried to pull together the layer upon layer of issues and intertwining events which impacted on decision-making about the Cyprus problem during the decade in question. Crucial to the strategy was the role that the EU could play in the search for the solution, given the desire of Cyprus, and come to that of Turkey, to join the EU. Turkey's influence could not be considered without detailed attention to the wider international community, and the vested interests of the US in particular. Then there is the vexed question of whether or not a solution is vital before Cyprus can enter the EU, and whether the British interest really is altruistic, or more likely a reflection of the importance of the intelligence facilities that Britain maintains on Cyprus. Critically, of course, is just how Turkey really figures in this process and whether the dialogue between George Papandreou and Ismail Cem begun after the devastating earthquakes in Turkey and Greece can make a difference. I have relived the painful struggle for the customs union with Turkey and tried to understand why Cyprus is only part of Turkey's problems. But perhaps the most important question of all is what is the real potential for stability in the eastern Mediterranean, and is Cyprus really the key to unlock that potential?

Cyprus is, without question, the main focus of the book. In beginning work I wrestled with the need to include a brief thumbnail history of Cyprus. However, knowing as I do that so much of the current impasse in a solution to the Cyprus problem is influenced by the semantics of the historical debate, I decided against getting embroiled in the politics of the past and to rely instead on the numerous accounts of the island's history that are already in print and cover every one of the various perspectives. So whilst Cyprus remains the focus, I have also tried to say something about the potential for the evolution of a new political infrastructure in Europe, about its pressure points and its weaknesses, and to discuss the interaction between Cyprus, Greece and Turkey and the role which Britain can play in influencing the future for Cyprus.

I wanted as well to demonstrate that if the EU is to have the political dynamism that it claims then it has to be able to act on issues in which it has a strong vested interest. The triangular relationship of Greece, Turkey and Cyprus presents a pre-eminent example of such an issue.

The greatest criticism of the EU and its institutions is that they are hidebound, bureaucratic and moribund. I wanted to change that perception by proving that the Parliament, the only truly democratic part of the EU structure, could and indeed did make a difference by developing new approaches, new initiatives and using its powers and rights to their limit in a challenging and innovative way. It pressed and questioned the European Council, harried and hassled the European Commission and made it submit to new controls and minute monitoring. The Parliament was central to the discussion and the decision-making on this issue.

The problem of Cyprus needs to be solved, and I wanted to make my contribution by using the EU to help that happen and happen speedily. On my retirement from the European Parliament at the beginning of 2000, Cyprus was well down the road of joining the EU; the problem had not been solved but there was a healthy international drive to make progress on the assumption that the problem could be resolved in conjunction with membership of the EU.

In writing this book, perhaps more than anything else I wanted to put in writing my strong support and admiration for those Cypriots, both Greek and Turkish, who believe in a shared and peaceful future and are working hard to achieve it for themselves, their children and grandchildren.

December 2002

Acknowledgements

We understood from the start of Pauline's international political career that the issue of Cyprus was of paramount concern for anyone who politically represented north London. We sought to take our own initiatives driven by a commitment to this political cause, rather than simply act as a cypher for the political motivations of others.

Much support, help and advice was received from the Cypriot community, both Greek and Turkish, in north London. Heartfelt, warm and fulsome thanks to the many Greek Cypriots who simply made contact to express their thanks and support. To the many Turkish Cypriots who got in touch to give pieces of news, guidance and ideas, we remain deeply touched by their courage and friendship in often difficult circumstances. If this book has been written for anyone, it is for them all.

There are many Greek and Turkish Cypriot and non-Cypriot colleagues in the Labour Party who have been amongst the most stalwart of supporters and collaborators.

We want to pay tribute to Hassan Raif, a tireless worker for and advocate of a distinct Turkish Cypriot identity and culture, and to Ilker Killich who, together with Hassan, changed the dynamics in the Turkish Cypriot community in London and made a real difference. I was glad to have the opportunity offered by London Turkish Radio in Wood Green to communicate with the Turkish-speaking community.

In the early years we received overwhelming help from George Ktorou and much friendship from his wife Stella and their children. We were deeply saddened when George decided to support another candidate in the European elections of 1999 in protest at the Labour Government's support for actions over Kosovo. His loss was a real one, but it couldn't diminish his earlier contribution.

We want to make special mention of Haris Sophoclides and his wife Diana. Both were tremendously supportive of our work and also that of other politicians who worked to end the division of Cyprus. Leonidas Leonidou of the EKEKA association was fundamental to our early understanding of the Cyprus issue. Thanks as well to Peter, our photographer over many years, George from London Greek Radio and Doros, always available with his television camera.

Amongst the diplomatic community in London, Brussels and Cyprus we are pleased to count many friends. We would mention just one, Nicos Agathocleous, former Ambassador of the Republic of Cyprus to the EU. Amongst his other distinctions, Nicos was the only man we know who accurately forecast the date of Margaret Thatcher's political demise!

Colleagues in the European Parliament are too many to mention, but our thanks are due to our close collaborator on the Cyprus issue the German SPD member of parliament, Mechtild Rothe. Mechtild never forgave Pauline, when as Leader of the Socialist Group she did not manage to secure the Chair of the Cyprus Joint Parliamentary Committee for her in January 1997. This is the opportunity to put in writing that that failure was the result of a disgraceful piece of dishonest manoeuvring by the Liberal Democrats in an attempt to hit Pauline where they knew it would hurt most. We were both upset and embarrassed by it!

In Cyprus itself, we have first and foremost to thank our comrades in the former socialist party EDEK. Whilst we were always keen to work with people from across the political spectrum, we were always clear about where we came from politically. Dr Vassos Lyssarides was an invaluable ally, someone whose analysis was always sought and whose contribution and views were greatly respected. We worked with two presidents of the Republic of Cyprus, Glafcos Clerides and George Vassiliou, both of whom were generous with time and never failed to make themselves available for discussion. We met regularly with the late Spyros Kyprianou and with Dimitris Christofias, as well as with many other political and parliamentary leaders. Perhaps the most personal relationships developed with the many friends in the Socialist Women movement (particularly as Ray married one of them!). Our thanks in particular to Roulla Mavronicola and Anna Yiannakou.

Amongst the Turkish Cypriot politicians whom we met over the years we would put Mehmet Ali Talat and Mustafa Akinci amongst the most powerful and stimulating. Discussions with both of them enabled us to keep abreast of the political sensitivities and views of the Turkish Cypriot community. We remain greatly in debt to them both; also to Alpay Durduran, whose personal dedication and radical commitment to the cause of Cyprus has put him at real personal risk on several occasions, and to Ozker Ozgur.

We met with many Greek Cypriots and Turkish Cypriots seeking an end to their island's trauma. Many continue to seek news of the final resting place of their missing family members. Others would love to go back to their homes, wherever they happen to be on the island. We want to end our thanks with the story of a young woman called Photini Charalambous, who wrote every year for 14 years, starting when she was still a child in junior school. She could not understand the length of time it was taking to find a solution. Photini and her peers are sadly growing up without knowledge and experience of their Turkish Cypriot compatriots.

A last tribute must be for the hard-working staff in London, particularly Christine Nation, Liz Mason, Joyce Sullivan, Mark Cottle and Richard Tomlinson, who over the years ran the constituency office and were the first port of call for members of both communities.

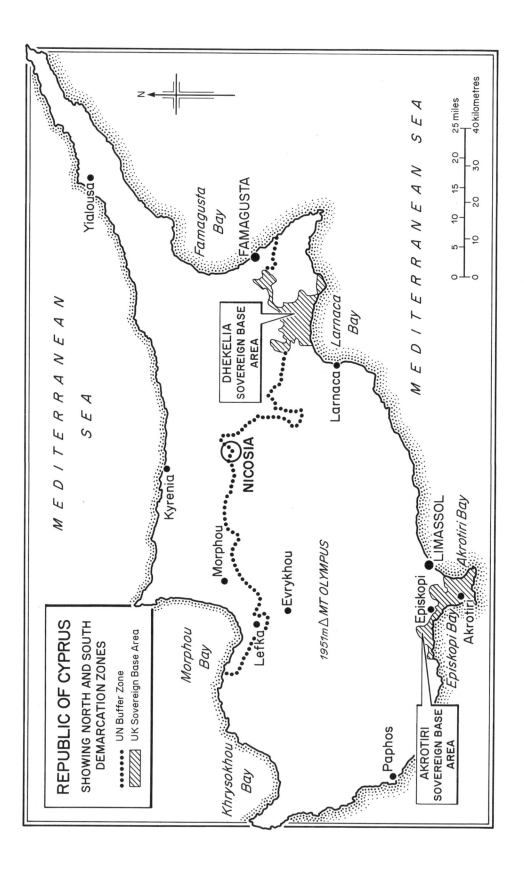

1   A strategy developed:

unity plus EU membership

By 1989 the island of Cyprus had been physically split into two for 15 years. In 1974, after many years of simmering and sometimes violent inter-communal discord, the Turkish army had invaded the north of the island. Their advance into the sovereign territory of Cyprus was facilitated by the stupendously ill-judged decision of the Greek military dictatorship to fund and support a coup in an attempt to overthrow the then President of Cyprus, Archbishop Makarios. The ultimate aim of the coup was to achieve 'Enosis' – union with Greece.

During the intervening years, the history of the island of Cyprus has been comprehensively documented from every conceivable angle in many studies, journals and books. In that context, I have not delved into its detail except where necessary to illustrate an issue or demonstrate a point. What was true, however, was that the EU (or the European Economic Community as it was then) played no significant part in the politics of Cyprus before and during 1974. Cyprus was not then a prospective member of the EEC, nor was it the significant economic regional player in the eastern Mediterranean that it subsequently became. At that stage Cyprus had not seriously contemplated membership of the club of Europe; indeed it was not even a twinkle in the eyes of the leading players in the European concept.

In the years since 1974, the problem of Cyprus had remained unresolved. The magnitude of the invasion and its impact on the

Cypriot people and for the region had been largely masked by two factors. They were the overriding dominance of the Middle East as an international focus in the region, particularly the Arab–Israeli conflict, and the fact that neither Greek nor Turkish Cypriot refugees were left to fester in the squalor of massive temporary tented camps, as had sadly become a common feature of modern-day refugee tragedies. Rather all Cypriots were rapidly housed: in the north through the sequestration of Greek Cypriot houses for those Turkish Cypriot refugees who had fled to the newly Turkish-controlled areas; in the south through a massive programme of house building that provided both accommodation and jobs for the one third of the Greek Cypriot community that had been forcibly displaced by the Turkish invasion. Whilst that effort was indisputably the right approach in human terms, it allowed the international community to present Cyprus as a low-level political and humanitarian problem.

What cannot be denied is that the problem of Cyprus was, on one level a real irritant complicating international relations with and for Turkey, and at its most pronounced remained a potential source of serious and dangerous conflict in an already considerably unstable part of the world. In a climate of long-standing inter-communal conflict in the Middle East and the more recent history in the Balkans, it was even more dangerous to consider the Cyprus problem as under control. The frustrations of factions in both communities, particularly amongst the refugee peoples, coupled with the coming to maturity of a generation of Greek and Turkish Cypriots completely unknown to each other, was a volatile mix.

Without doubt the problem of Cyprus was multi-faceted, complex and did not lend itself to a simple thumbnail sketch. It was also true that there was no one single victim, neither individual nor community. Nor was there one single side with whom all truth and honour resided. All who had engaged in the cause of the re-unification of the island of Cyprus recognized the objective truth that there had been faults on both sides, and that abuses and tragedies were suffered by each community at the hands of the other. The long-standing stalemate owed much to an argument of degree. Who suffered most? Correspondingly, who was to blame most? Who was the victim? And, therefore, who was the aggressor?

That this was a sterile and unproductive debate had been recognized by most who sought to help find a solution. The forced division of the island understandably remained most difficult to acknowledge for those whose lives, families and futures remained blighted. The unnatural division and continuing dislocation of ordinary discourse between Greek Cypriots and Turkish Cypriots was and remains a human tragedy.

The underlying motivation of those of us in the European institutions who believed that the Cyprus problem needed to be solved, and that the European Parliament offered one forum for opening up the debate, was that the status quo on Cyprus was both dangerous and unsustainable. What needed to happen was a convergence of like-minded individuals from both communities determined to secure a solution. However, recourse to simple confidence-building exercises between common interest groups of Greek and Turkish Cypriots was not enough. Such exercises could only ever have flourished in the context of real acts of political will. This would have created an environment in which those confidence-building measures provided the opportunity to drive the process forward.

It was in that context and environment that I articulated a single strategic political objective that has become the crux of the discussion and decision-making on the Cyprus problem in the EU since that time. The political objective was that the unity of Cyprus could, for the foreseeable future, only be achieved through the accession of the entire island to the EU.

In 1989 a small dedicated team of politicians, support staff and advisers began work in the European Parliament to enshrine this principle as the fundamental concept on which the EU would establish its future relationship with Cyprus.

Coterminous with this went equally important work to reinvigorate the issue with national decision-makers and political parties in the Member States of the EU, and to establish the European Parliament as a key player in the eyes of the protagonists in the eastern Mediterranean, both civil and military.

By 1994 the first phase of that work had been completed. In the search for a solution to the Cyprus problem, the European Parliament as an institution had become a political agitator that simply could not be circumnavigated by national politicians or

European bureaucrats. By that time, the group of parliamentarians who supported the concept had grown in size and commitment, covering all the political groupings in the European Parliament and all the nationalities in the EU.

The second phase began in the middle of 1994, when the European elections and the constitution of the fourth directly elected European Parliament offered new political opportunities. In particular, I was elected to the most senior political post in the Parliament, that of Leader of the Parliamentary Group of the Party of European Socialist/Social Democrats (more usually known as the Socialist Group), then the largest political grouping in the European Parliament. That same political family rapidly moved to become the leading political grouping in governments across Europe. This was completed in 1997 by the switch in political balance in the EU from right to left following the general elections in the UK, France and Germany.

The first sense that life in the EU was about to change reverberated around the bi-annual congress of the Socialist Group in June 1997. Earlier congresses of the European socialists had hardly set the world alight, press interest had always been limited and policy direction was not usually on the agenda in any serious way. This congress, six weeks after the election of Tony Blair and New Labour in Britain, and just 14 days after the election of Lionel Jospin and the socialists in France, was different. It took place in Malmö, Sweden, and hundreds of journalists lined up for accreditation once it was announced that both Blair and Jospin would attend and speak together on a common platform at a public session.

Activity on the fringes of the congress was frantic as the aides of the two newly elected prime ministers tried to ensure that their man secured the best slot. Who was to come onto the congress platform first? Which one was to speak first and for how long? But, as the battle went on for ephemeral advantage, the real issue was lost. Nobody was concerning themselves with the need to secure a degree of consensus on what the two party leaders would actually say. In the event, Jospin gave a speech interpreted by the press as a traditional socialist, interventionist approach, characterized in UK terms as 'old Labour'. Tony Blair on the other hand developed his 'third way', modernize or die, 'New Labour' appeal on the European platform.

With hindsight that first and crucial public meeting was a defining moment for social-democratic leadership in Europe. The lack of coherence opened up a wound which the press and our political opponents continued to pick at during the ensuing years.

But although the history of the EU's development was set to change with the swing to social-democratic leadership, the story of the way in which the remarkably successful campaign for Cyprus was orchestrated illustrated the possibilities offered by the new politics of the EU, its institutions and its relationships with the governments of its Member States. It identified the scope for opening up international decision-making, and demonstrated that those engaged in the politics of the EU needed to understand better their cross-border environment if they were to innovate and develop new approaches for the conduct of politics at a European level, rather than simply aping the formalities, traditions and handicaps of national decision-making.

During the heady days following the signing of the Oslo Accords between Israeli and Palestinian leaders, that remarkable Israeli double act of Prime Minister Yitzak Rabin and his Foreign Minister Shimon Peres said often that Israelis and Palestinians would never agree on the past, but they could agree on a shared vision for the future. It requires a certain sort of leadership to carry through that approach in a situation and environment of tension, deep-rooted hostility and total mistrust and suspicion.

Likewise Cypriots will never agree on their past. Cyprus needed to begin the painful process of drawing a line under its recent history. This does not mean forgiving or forgetting what had happened. It does not entail dismissing the past. It does, however, mean recognizing that if tomorrow's Cypriots are to have a future without deep-rooted tensions and hatreds, then the current generations of both communities are required to undertake the supreme act of generosity. That generosity need not be directed towards the other community, but rather towards their own children and grandchildren. Succeeding generations must be able to see that their parents' pain, whilst real and deeply felt, had not been allowed to mar their opportunity to inherit a united, free and peace-loving Cyprus.

Greek Cypriots and Turkish Cypriots need the space and stability to start developing that shared vision of the future. It cannot be on Greek Cypriot terms or Turkish Cypriot terms. It must be truly shared. No amount of poring over earlier legal agreements, unworkable constitutions, unrecorded conversations and broken promises will end the division of Cyprus. An act of will is required by all parties to decide that the time has come for peace.

The international community had a responsibility to help. In the context of Cyprus, the UN had exercised that responsibility since 1964 and made many valiant attempts to bring the two sides together. The major players and certainly the major stakeholders in securing peace and reconciliation in Cyprus were, however, all European countries. Greece, Turkey and the UK have had a special relationship with Cyprus, having accepted the responsibility of 'Guarantor Powers' under the 1960 Constitution and Treaty of Guarantee. That Treaty of Guarantee laid on Greece, Turkey and the UK the role of guaranteeing 'the maintenance of the independence, territorial integrity, security and respect for the constitution of the Republic of Cyprus'.

Whilst the responsibility for securing a solution had been in the hands of the UN for some four decades, there was no question that the answer lay in Europe. After the more recent experiences in Bosnia, Kosovo and Macedonia there can surely be no-one left in Europe who would not concede that if Cyprus were to become a live conflict into which Greece and Turkey were inevitably drawn then the European states would have to use their powers to intervene. Those powers could be drawn from NATO, but that would be considerably complicated with both Greece and Turkey being full members. Negotiating their agreement for NATO action to intervene in a conflict between them could prove nigh impossible. The EU would, of course, be able to seek to activate its capacity through the European Security and Defence Policy (ESDP). This, however, would almost certainly be seen as a hostile act by Turkey, if it remained outside the ESDP and antagonistic to it. So it would be down to a handful of countries to exercise leadership and intervene politically, diplomatically and even militarily to avoid the destabilization of the region and ultimately the wider continent.

The division of Cyprus was and always had been a European issue. During the Cold War era the Western democracies quite deliberately sought to ignore that reality. The priority in that period was clear, to give succour to a US agenda that concentrated on strategic arms balance with the Soviet Union, based on an un-spoken recognition of spheres of influence. Turkey was strategically important to the US. In that context, therefore, Cyprus as an issue did not even feature on any scale of US interests, with the exception of its clear priority to ensure that the British main-tained the intelligence facilities which they had developed on Cyprus. The outcome from this intelligence capacity was shared with the US and gave it a valuable insight into Soviet nuclear and missile testing capabilities. With the British presence on Cyprus secure, the US remained confident that the troubles on Cyprus presented no immediate or real threat to the British presence or the intelligence facilities. Hence US allies in Europe correspond-ingly allowed the issue of Cyprus to stagnate and sink down the political agenda.

There are those who continue to argue that to allow Cyprus to join the EU would be to import an intractable problem into the EU. History seems to indicate that those holding such a view either have an alternative, unspoken agenda, or are simply being disingenuous. A conflict between Greeks and Turks on or over Cyprus would be a conflict that the EU and its Member States simply could not ignore, and into which they would inevitably be drawn. Cyprus has always been a European problem.

The UN can justifiably point to a series of genuine and hard-worked initiatives and proposals, and hours of time spent in head-to-head or proximity discussions with the leaders of the Greek and Turkish Cypriot communities. However, absolutely no progress was made towards the establishment of a reunified Cyprus with a robust constitution respecting the rights of all Cypriots, and recognizing the essential contribution of both communities to the future health, prosperity and success of the state.

The UN had identified the issues that needed to be addressed. In doing this they had also found viable solutions to those issues that divided the two communities. Using the framework of a bi-zonal, bi-communal federation agreed by the leaders of both communities at high-level talks brokered by the UN in 1977, the definition of the territorial size of the two federated states had been minutely explored and largely resolved. The crucial issues of the collective and individual security of both communities had been addressed by imaginative proposals for de-militarization and by significant international support for any necessary transitional phase. The thorny problem of the return of the refugees to their homes had been broached with detailed proposals for the early reopening to both communities of the ghost city of Famagusta and the return of Greek Cypriot refugees to their traditional homes in the town of Morphou and its surrounding villages. Both of these actions, it was assumed, would over time generate significant trust and goodwill in both communities. Several robust international examples had already been used to draw up a constitution and a political structure for a federal Cyprus that gave shape and structure to both the federal state and its constituent parts.

The solution sat neatly packaged, if largely untouched, on shelves in New York. But the UN had always lacked the single ingredient that traditionally drives such negotiations to a conclusion. What was missing was that ingredient that creates the friction and tension to motivate those involved to secure agreement. That ingredient was leverage. The UN always had to rely only on the persuasive strength of its arguments, its proposals, the personalities behind them, and the backing of the UN Security Council. It had never had direct leverage of any significance.

Of itself, the UN would still not have leverage. The EU provided the missing ingredient. The quite remarkable development of the EU since the mid-to-late 1980s, from a tired old regional economic grouping into a dynamic global economic and political entity, had exponentially heightened its attraction to the states around its borders. From Finland to Malta and from Poland to Turkey, the older and newer European states had lined up to enter the EU. They came for a variety of reasons and a complex of motivations, but come they did with a clear desire to be part of the European project. The EU that jumped from 12 to 15 Member States on 1 January 1995 when Sweden, Finland and Austria joined, will virtually double the number of its members when the next 10 candidate states enter in May 2004.

With both Cyprus and Turkey set on the road to membership of the EU, the dynamics of the solution to the Cyprus problem changed. The EU had always supported the UN's role in the hunt for a solution to the political problem of Cyprus. Even with its more recent and enhanced engagement in the issue as a direct result of the application of Cyprus to join the Union, it continued to support the UN as the vital international mediator in the process. It did not seek to usurp that role, nor to interfere in its management. What it did do was to offer some key new perspectives, and an international framework within which the solution would sit. As well as that, the drive towards membership of the EU also offered a tight timetable that unquestionably focused the minds of all participants.

In advancing the argument that entry to the EU would be a catalyst to the solution of the problem of Cyprus, I had always argued that the two processes would run in parallel. There were those who argued that Cyprus's membership of the EU should not happen until either Turkey joined the EU at the same time, or until a solution to the Cyprus problem had been found.

In some circumstances these two arguments could be regarded as either persuasive or sensible, or both. The first is comprehensively discussed later. The latter argument was deeply flawed, posited as it was on the continuation of the status quo, or at worst the formal division of the island into two separate states.

The continuation of the status quo meant that the informal partition of the island, which had led to Cyprus being one of the most heavily militarized countries in the world, would have continued for an indeterminate period. This would have left Cyprus as a potential trouble-spot in the eastern Mediterranean, with all the attendant dangers. The international community had a responsibility to do all it could to eliminate a problem that was potentially the cause of a military conflict in an already turbulent region. The problem also remained a constant and continuing irritant in relations between Greece and Turkey, and a potential cause of military conflict between them. It posed, therefore, a significant hindrance to attempts to generate greater understanding between these two major powers in the region. It also presented a real difficulty for the prospect of Turkish membership of the EU.

If it were accepted that Cyprus should not join the EU until after a solution, it is clear to see that the imperative to seek a solution would be lost. After all, decades of detailed and painstaking work by the UN had resulted in absolutely no change. What would be different without the clear commitment of the EU to bring Cyprus into the European family and the clearly defined timetable towards that cause? Where would the incentive be for a resolution to the problem? To accept such a position would be unequivocally to have removed the leverage and momentum that was in the hands of the international peace brokers, and impoverish the UN process once more. Not only would that have damaged the best interests of Cypriots and their long-term future, but it would also have been a devastatingly lost opportunity.

A great many of those arguing for the 'solution first' model also argued that before a solution could be found the international community would have to recognize two separate states in Cyprus. This was the demand of the Turkish Cypriot leadership in the closing years of the 1990s and the beginning of 2000. It bedevilled the UN process through the opening years of the new millennium. Such a demand represented a back-tracking from the position to which both sides had put their signature in 1977. It was used as the basis for the withdrawal of Rauf Denktash, the Turkish Cypriot leader, from talks in Geneva and New York. This is a critical point and one that requires attention.

Since 1974, the UN had navigated a careful way around the sensitive issue of recognition by inviting to the talks the recognized leader of each of the Cypriot communities, rather than dealing with official titles and office holders. As the Security Council and the General Assembly of the UN had from day one recognized only one sovereign government on Cyprus, that of the Republic of Cyprus, this formula, accepted by both communities, was both pragmatic and sensible.

The attempts to alter the basis on which negotiations had been conducted since 1974, and insist on the recognition of a separate sovereignty on Cyprus, raised suspicions and anxiety about motivations. As a tactic, it appears to have had no objective other than to delay and stall talks, rather than expedite them. Amongst the most vociferous in criticism of this move were Turkish Cypriot opposition political leaders themselves, who argued that this step had left Turkish Cypriots with no voice and no opportunity to influence events. They urged their own leaders to return to the negotiating table.

As far as the EU was concerned, it had always accepted the UN resolutions as the basis for its formal relations with Cyprus. This meant that it recognized the right of the Republic of Cyprus to apply for membership of the EU. However, it sought to work with the administration of the Republic to secure an invitation for the Turkish Cypriot community to take part in the process of negotiating membership of the Union. That invitation, brokered by British Prime Minister Tony Blair and his Foreign Secretary Robin Cook at a side meeting during the Commonwealth Heads of Government meeting in Edinburgh in October 1997, was rejected by the Turkish Cypriot leadership, which argued that membership of the EU was not possible for Cyprus until Turkey too entered.

Those tempted to go down the 'solution first' route reject the argument that the dynamic created by the 'parallel course' model offers a window of opportunity. However, such a model is designed to run talks for a solution alongside, and on an identical timetable to, talks on membership of the Union, with the real expectation that both would be completed together. This maximizes the synergy and support available from both processes, for both processes. The solutions to the Cyprus problem and membership of the EU would thus reinforce and sustain each other and optimizes the opportunity for success.

The entry of any country to the EU is a long, detailed and often tedious process. To use the word 'negotiations' in the context of entry to the Union is something of a misnomer. The Union's 'acquis communautaire', its 80,000 pages of legislation, have to be adopted by the candidate country. There is no negotiation about that fact. The negotiations relate to the speed of adoption and any necessary transitional arrangements, where there are particular problems of implementation in a candidate state. That process is technical and administrative and is carried out largely by the civil service of the candidate country and the bureaucracy of the European Commission.

The EU is certainly based on the rule of law, and governed by its Treaty provisions. It is, however, not just a legal body. It has a dynamic political apex. That political apex, the European Council, can and frequently does assume the responsibility, the right and the duty to seek political solutions to problems. Over the years it had exercised this role both between its Member States and internationally.

Such political issues, which certainly exist for every candidate country, are the subject of high-level contacts between the government of the applicant state and the members of the European

Commission, that is the 20 European Commissioners themselves, in close concert with the European Council of Ministers, and are subject to final ratification by the European Parliament and the national parliaments of Member States.

What is clear is that the European Council and Commission have the capacity to seek political agreements outside of the adoption of the acquis communautaire to expedite and facilitate entry of any country should they deem it necessary or desirable. For instance, at their accession, Spain and Portugal were denied access to the totality of the Common Fisheries Policy for a full 15 years, given the problems already being experienced with fish stocks in European waters, and the consequent threat presented to the existing EU fishing communities by the large fishing fleets of both countries. A further example is to be found during the entry of Finland. The European Council invented a whole new policy and associated funding regime to support the northern Finnish forestry and rural economy that had suffered very badly following the collapse of the Soviet Union and the impact of new technologies on its paper-making industry.

It was in this political dimension that the scope lay for facilitating the progress to the solution of the problem of Cyprus. Naturally it would be important that in any political agreements that might be made the decision-makers keep a weather eye on what was practicable and sensible, particularly as any such agreement would need to be ratified by the European Parliament and thereafter by national parliaments throughout the Union.

Hence, with regard to Cyprus, the EU kept in regular contact with the UN on progress in the inter-communal talks on the solution. If both processes were to culminate at a predestined point which provided a solution to the Cyprus problem, taking as its centre Cyprus's membership of the EU, then the EU must give assurances that the shape of the solution did not contravene the acquis communautaire. Or, where it did, the proposed arrangements had to be within the scope of transitional arrangements as understood by the EU. It followed, therefore, that whilst no blank cheques could be given it was possible that in order to enhance or sustain some of the provisions of the solution they could be tailored to benefit from EU membership, for example in the areas of free movement of capital, goods, services and people.

The advocates of Cyprus's entry to the EU had always argued the case for parallelism between the solution to the Cyprus problem and entry to the EU. It had been stated many times that the preferred option of the EU was for Cyprus to join the Union as a united country, with both Greek and Turkish Cypriots playing their part in that relationship. It was clear in the statement following the decision made by the General Affairs Council of the EU (the Foreign Ministers of each Member State) on 6 March 1995 that the entry of Cyprus to the EU should not be blocked by the failure to find a solution to the Cyprus problem. The Helsinki Council declaration in 1999 went on to say:

> The European Council underlines that a political settlement will facilitate the accession of Cyprus to the EU. If no settlement has been reached by the completion of accession negotiations, the Council's decision on accession will be made without the above being a precondition. In this the Council will take account of all the relevant factors.

The only equivocation in that statement is the very last line. The significance of that final, almost throwaway, statement is huge, particularly given the attempts in some quarters since to create ambiguity around it. The Council of the EU was trying once again to ensure that it gave no licence to either party deliberately to be obstructive, whilst offering both parties the prospect of support for a constructive attitude. Hence the opening statement gave strong support to the application of the Government of Cyprus for entry, whilst making clear to the Denktash leadership that it had a window of opportunity which would last probably three or four years to make progress on a solution. At the same time it gave out the clear message to the Clerides Government that whilst there was support for Cyprus in the EU, if it attempted to use its pathway of entry to the EU to play hard to get on a solution, the Council's positive decision could not be taken for granted. It also made clear to Denktash that the behaviour of the Greek Cypriots was under constant and close examination and that he had the opportunity to influence the solution if he genuinely desired to and if he was prepared to take advantage of the moment. And so the situation remained.

2 Hand in hand with the UN:

Europe's guarantees for peace

Making the assumption that any solution to the Cyprus problem would take the shape already indicated by UN resolutions, what are the main provisions of the EU framework that could facilitate or support the solution to the Cyprus problem?

Security presented the first major problem with which the UN mediators were confronted.

The Turkish Cypriot community in the north of Cyprus, as the numerically smaller community, had an understandably strong sense of its potential insecurity and danger should the physical barrier between itself and the Greek Cypriot community be removed, or should the Turkish armed forces return to Turkey or be reduced to the levels agreed in the original Constitution. That fear has undoubtedly been exacerbated by decades of total separation from Greek Cypriots and given added impetus and gravitas in recent years by the inter-communal conflicts in the Balkans. That fear must be handled with the utmost vigour and rigour in any settlement. If Turkish Cypriots are to support a solution, they must be given unequivocal guarantees of their personal and collective security that carry weight and engender confidence, and are underpinned by the strength of the international community.

Greek Cypriots feel a sense of insecurity because of the close proximity of Cyprus to Turkey, and at the ease and speed with which Turkish military might has been demonstrated and exercised on Cyprus. In their view, the presence of the Turkish armed forces in the north of Cyprus has been an ever-present reminder of the potential Turkish military threat to the whole island. Any solution will need to deal with that sense of threat as well.

The importance of the EU's contribution to the security issue is that it offers security for every Cypriot. The 35,000 Turkish troops in the north of Cyprus offer security to just one section of the population, and leaves the other feeling considerably less secure. EU involvement in the peace process would have no such constraint. Its remit, its structures and its approach would be non-discriminatory. The EU could play a part through its growing defence and security role in supporting any provisions put in place by the UN.

But by far the most dramatic and far-reaching solution to these problems would be the demilitarization of the island. The Greek Cypriot and Turkish Cypriot armed forces on the island, along with the Turkish and Greek contingents, could be replaced, for as long as was necessary, by an international civil security system working with the indigenous civil policing provisions put in place under the terms of the solution. If the UN were playing the leading role, and the EU committed itself to provide the necessary policing support, the EU could be seen to be playing a positive and supportive role. Any such provision would clearly either have to exclude Greece from any EU personnel provision, or to include Turkish personnel as well.

The EU expectations of the necessary financial support for Cyprus, even with an additional and specific scheme for the development of the indigenous Turkish Cypriot economy, are tiny by comparison to the money the EU must make available to support the economies of the large candidate countries of Central and Eastern Europe. For the EU to provide an additional financial resource in support of an enhanced civil security system in a post-solution Cyprus could hardly represent an onerous financial burden given the stability and confidence it would engender in Cyprus and in the region.

The concept of a demilitarized Cyprus was proposed by Clerides after his election as President of the Republic of Cyprus in 1993. Denktash, on behalf of the Turkish Cypriots, rejected the proposal as it was then presented. However, at that point in the history of the inter-communal talks the overall package of measures for the security of the island and its citizens was not actively on the table or subject to imminent discussion by the two leaders. Such a proposal deserves to be reconsidered in the context of the solution. Needless to say, the proposal will need to take cognizance of the long-term strategic importance of the British military and intelligence capacity on the island if it is to have a serious prospect of success.

As Cyprus has been one of the most heavily militarized parts of the world, a solution that removed the threat of armed conflict from present and future generations of Cypriots could only be beneficial. Similarly, in the situation of a newly united Cyprus it would give entirely the right signals to both communities if the fortifications were dismantled and the weapons removed. It would also, of course, remove a source of potential weaponry during any subsequent difficult moments. No-one can deny that the potential for inter-communal conflict would remain into the foreseeable future, particularly as both communities sought to work through the new situation, developing their role and rights, and working within new constitutional structures.

The second issue revolves around the equal rights of all the citizens of Cyprus, regardless of ethnic origin. Here the EU offers two major benefits to its citizens.

Firstly, it provides a clear constitutional and legislative frame-work of rights based on European values, particularly as set out in the Charter of Fundamental Rights of the EU. Citizens, through petition to the European Parliament, by complaint to the European Commission, and in the final analysis by application to the European Court of Justice, can seek and find remedy for the abuse of those rights. There already exists a body of case law establishing the value of the Court of Justice and its judgments in support of minorities, anti-discrimination practices and equal opportunities within the EU. A great many of the successful cases have been won by citizens taking action for an infringement of their rights as a European citizen, against their own government, at national, regional or local level.

Secondly, the great strength of this constitutional, legislative and judicial framework in the case of Cyprus would be that it offers all citizens a clear and direct right of appeal in the event of their rights being denied or abused by the authorities of either federated or federal state.

By way of example, there are some Turkish Cypriots who decided to remain in their homes in the area controlled by the Government of the Republic of Cyprus after 1974, or who have returned to those homes in recent years. Some of them have had cause to complain about harassment by the police of the Republic of Cyprus. In a Cyprus located within the EU, with citizens able to access the legislative and administrative functions of the EU, they would have the right of appeal to an independent arbiter in defence of their rights.

Similarly, the Greek Cypriots living in the Karpas peninsula in the northern part of Cyprus, who have long been campaigning for their human and civil rights (documented by the Council of Europe's Barsony Report [Doc. 7717] of 1997) would have to be given the same rights as those guaranteed to Turkish Cypriots living within a Turkish Cypriot federated state. They too would have the security of appeal to the institutions of the EU and its constitutional and legislative framework.

The EU, by working in close partnership with those in the UN framing the proposals for the solution to the Cyprus problem, would be able to give a measure of comfort to both Greek Cypriots and Turkish Cypriots that there existed an independent recourse for them in the event of any future problems. This, of course, depends crucially on the willing endorsement of the leaders of the two communities that their domestic rights would be enshrined by recourse to the European framework of rights and the European Court of Justice. For Greece and Turkey it should be a relatively easy matter to encourage and endorse such an approach. Greece is already a member of the Union and subject to the jurisdiction of the Court of Justice in these matters. Turkey is on the road to membership of the EU and will have to undertake identical commitments.

The third issue is that of free movement of people.

The introduction of the European Single Act in February 1986 established four freedoms within the EU. They were the free movement of capital, goods, services and people. The aim was not to encourage mass migration of people, but to facilitate the maximum efficiency of the European economy in a rapidly changing world economic environment. Free movement of people guaranteed European citizens from one country the same rights as those of European citizens in any country within the EU in which they worked. To be clear, a European citizen does not transport his domestic rights with him from country to country; rather if a German citizen moved from Germany to Spain to work, he would have the same rights as a Spanish citizen and so on.

A major part of the Cyprus problem has been the issue of free movement. In the few short weeks of the war in 1974 hundreds of thousands of Cypriots were displaced, either forcibly, or through fear, or because of the ceasefire agreements at the conclusion of the conflict. No movement has been possible since that time for Greek Cypriots wishing to return to their homes in the north, and whilst the border remains open for Turkish Cypriots in the other direction only a limited number have chosen to return to the former Turkish Cypriot villages in the south. The relaxation of that restraint is contentious. Greek Cypriots greatly desire that freedom, and whilst a proportion of the Turkish Cypriots would relish it as well, there remains an understandable sense of fear and insecurity within the smaller Turkish Cypriot community about their physical safety in that totally open border situation.

It is perfectly feasible that in any proposed solution this issue would be subject to a transitional period during which trust and confidence would have to be established between the two communities. This would undoubtedly be subject to the ebb and flow of individual grievances and sensitivities and would be likely, therefore, to be the area of greatest stress after any solution. The examples of the continuing inter-community tension in the post-ceasefire Northern Ireland and the calamitous relapse to even greater violence in Israel and Palestine are testimony to the delicate nature of post-conflict community relations.

Any appropriate UN transitional measures developed to help both communities to clear that hurdle over a period of time could certainly be accommodated within the framework of transitional arrangements for membership of the EU. Joint UN and EU monitoring of the working of such transitional arrangements could offer reassurances that individuals were being treated properly and any difficulties were being fairly handled. The ultimate aim over time would be to develop the domestic confidence to move to a situation in which Cyprus became a truly European state embracing the concept of free movement open to all EU citizens within the administration of both federated states.

The EU could, therefore, be the facilitator of that process, and perhaps with the UN and other agreed partners could even be the vehicle for regular assessments as to when the time was right to move to the next step in the process.

The fourth issue is that of the economic regeneration of the north of the island.

Those opposing EU entry often claim that supporters of membership of the EU have tried to buy Turkish Cypriot support by offering EU funds for agriculture and the regeneration of the economy of the north of the island in general.

The Turkish Cypriots would unquestionably be major economic beneficiaries of the entry of a united Cyprus into the EU. Their economy has been totally dependent on Turkey since 1974. This has created considerable difficulties during the period in which the Turkish economy experienced hyperinflation and economic down-turn. The problems were compounded by the collapse of some significant businesses, coupled with the international ban on exports from the north of the island. The fact that the Turkish Cypriot administration is itself the major employer further exacerbates the problem. This has resulted in Turkey being required to inject large amounts of cash to sustain such employment. In 2001, the per-capita income in the north of the island was €5000, compared to €19,250 in the territory controlled by the Government of the Republic.

The EU practice in the rest of Europe has been to direct any aid and support towards those regions in most need. Given the obvious disparity in wealth between north and south, the overwhelming input from the European funding regimes would be spent in the north for the benefit of the Turkish Cypriots. The Government of the Republic of Cyprus has recognized that reality.

In this context the EU is ill served by its own complex procedures and far from transparent decision-making processes. Layer upon layer of administrative checks and counter-checks promote a sense of a dense and deliberately obscure bureaucracy. It need not be so. It might just help move the debate forward if it was more widely understood how the EU currently organizes the distribution of its funding regimes. What is important is the basis for the use of EU monies and how these funds would be delivered and controlled.

A study of the present systems for the distribution of EU money demonstrates that the bureaucracy of the Union retains certain rights over authorization of the projects on which EU funding is spent. Each EU Member State is divided into internal regions, and it is planned that Cyprus would be no exception – the natural regional differentiation being between the Greek Cypriot federated state and the Turkish Cypriot federated state in the context of a federal solution. Not only does such a regional structure make good sense in the political, administrative and community context, but in terms of economic and social conditions the two proposed federated states are currently very different, with their own specific features and problems.

Each region of the EU that receives money from European spending programmes must first present a regional programme, which is then collated into a national programme. Once Brussels accepts the national programme each region provides a detailed action plan of its proposed spending, including the national and regional administrative and bureaucratic structures in place to oversee its implementation. The action plans must demonstrate how the diverse interests such as business, community, voluntary sector and regional authorities are represented in the process of decision-making and implementation. These arrangements, already in place and operating in the existing EU Member States, should give confidence that EU financing would largely be in the hands of regions to spend on programmes agreed directly by the EU. That would be the position even before consideration was to be given to any specific provisions for a newly united Cyprus.

As well as the clear potential for the north of the island to benefit from the funding regime, the Union would seek to put in place a special programme for Cyprus. In a private discussion with Günter Verheugen, the member of the European Commission responsible for enlargement, he made clear that the EU programme for peace and reconciliation that was made available to Northern Ireland as a direct consequence of the ceasefire and peace process in that country would provide a guide to just what could be done for Cyprus. The peace and reconciliation fund in Northern Ireland was used extensively for cross-community contacts and reconciliation. Directed towards community groups coming together to deal with tensions and difficulties, there are countless examples of projects of excellence that could show the way for something similar in Cyprus.

The other recognized fear is of economic paternalism, that in a period when the Turkish Cypriot economy would be under great stress its businesses would be easy and lucrative pickings for the sophisticated Greek Cypriot business world. The issue of economic paternalism remains a sensitive one. The EU's economic philosophy has moved sharply to that of a social market economy that invests in human resources and technological strengths in order to be well placed to succeed as part of an advanced technological global future. The Republic of Cyprus has many recognized strengths in this respect, and membership of the Union can be expected to bring some rewards for its highly motivated and skilled workforce. To intervene in that market process has been generally frowned upon in the EU. However, in a situation where Cyprus has secured a solution to its national problem and where there is much EU support directed to business regeneration in the north of the island, it is perfectly conceivable that the criteria for spending programmes in Cyprus should stipulate specific support for indigenous Turkish Cypriot businesses.

Such action would have the aim of not just regenerating economic life in the north, but of giving direct sustenance to the solution by stimulating Turkish Cypriot confidence, growing that community's businesses, and limiting the disproportionate disadvantage in the economic life of the country which it might otherwise suffer.

In overall terms, the bringing together of the solution to the Cyprus problem and membership of the Union would unlock the true potential of the economic strength of the island. The underdevelopment of the north represents a missed opportunity for Cypriots. Fifty-three per cent of the coastline – one of the most sought-after coastlines in the Mediterranean tourist industry – lies within the area controlled by the Turkish army. It also contains some of the most fertile agricultural land in Cyprus, the Messaoria Plain. Thus the funding regimes of the EU would give a huge boost to the rapid development of the north of the island, tempered, of course, by environmental and planning safeguards.

All of this has to be seen in the context of the growing regionalization of the EU. In its early decades through to the mid-1980s, the structure of the EU and its overwhelmingly centralized Member States would not have offered an attractive option for Cyprus.

With the development of its political identity, the EU now offers the opportunity for developing synergy and support for the solution to the problem of Cyprus. With its increasingly decentralized and regionalized shape and geography, a federal Cyprus very definitely has an opportunity to maximize its impact as a united country in the political structures of the EU. At the same time it could enjoy significant levels of economic autonomy, devolved to its federated states, through EU regeneration, support packages and systems.

As well as the four major areas identified above, there are numerous other ways in which EU membership would facilitate the implementation of a solution by establishing joint action for the good of the entire community, for instance on the environment, on joint research and health projects, or youth and women's programmes.

These are quintessentially projects that impact on the everyday lives of citizens. This begs the question of whether or not the people of Cyprus generally support membership of the EU and what it offers.

Unquestionably amongst the Greek Cypriots there has been a strong and steady trend in favour of membership of the Union. In its 2001 survey of public views on the EU and their country's membership application, Eurobarometer, the most advanced and sophisticated market-research tool into EU trends, found that there was clear support for EU membership, with 51 per cent of the 500 Greek Cypriots surveyed strongly in favour, 62 per cent indicating that they would support their country's membership of the EU in a referendum. Eurobarometer's deeper analysis of that figure showed that 72 per cent of the 500 Greek Cypriots would have voted 'yes' if a referendum had been conducted at that moment. A surprisingly large percentage of Greek Cypriots, in fact some 62 per cent, also trusted the institutions of the EU.

So despite the delays and difficulties, Greek Cypriots still have a positive view on the accession of their country to the EU. The majority of them expect that Cyprus will gain a lot from it. According to a survey of Greek Cypriots conducted by RAI Consultancy Services Ltd working on behalf of Cyprobarometer for the Planning and Economic Research Service of the Laiki Banking Group, the most important benefit from the accession to the EU was felt to be that of economic development. The second important benefit, with significantly less popularity than the first, was national security.

Membership of the EU would have a distinct advantage for Greek Cypriots if it secured reunification of the island, and, so the argument of the critics goes, they would want it, wouldn't they! The answer to that must clearly be yes. This is, without doubt, one of the major motivations for the political parties and the leadership of the country. From their perspective this ranks as a perfectly legitimate motivation. If the EU can help to resolve a situation which the entire world, as reflected in the UN, believes must be resolved, every effort should be used to harness that potential.

However, it is too simplistic to apply such a stereotypical motivation to the entire Greek Cypriot community. Over the last 20 years, the economy of Cyprus has flourished. Greek Cypriots have a record of success in higher education and are acknowledged for their use of high levels of technological sophistication. They have established the Republic of Cyprus as a regional banking and business centre of some considerable significance in the eastern Mediterranean. The business and finance world would like to be part of the EU for the benefits they see for themselves in business terms, of being part of the largest single market in the world, particularly as it expands into Central and Eastern Europe, in which many of their businesses are already deeply engaged and financially committed.

Young Turkish Cypriots and Greek Cypriots are excited by the prospect of being part of one of the most innovative and inspirational ventures in the world. They also understand the opportunities it offers them for education, free movement, cultural exchange, experience and work. Their main motivation is to secure a part in this new world.

For other citizens, both Greek Cypriot and Turkish Cypriot, there is motivation in the concept of a Europe that is seeking to bring together countries that have fought each other for years. Within the EU as it exists at the moment are nation states that have been bitter enemies for centuries. Germany, Britain and France for instance have not had such a sustained period of peace between themselves for centuries. Nobody ever said it would be an easy task to bring these countries together. There are clearly problems and difficulties all the way down the road, but these problems are now shared around a table instead of resolved on the fields of war. For tens of thousands of Greek Cypriots and Turkish Cypriots, that message has a crystal clear resonance – 'Why not us?' they ask. That is not the voice of cynicism; it is the voice of hope and goodwill.

According to Turkish Cypriot politicians and the media and press in the north of Cyprus, the overwhelming majority of Turkish Cypriots in the north of the island are in favour of membership of the EU. An opinion poll carried out in the north of Cyprus between 2 and 4 October 2001 and published in the Turkish Cypriot newspaper *Halkin Sesi* reported that 93.3 per cent of those questioned favoured Cyprus's accession to the EU. Interestingly, the same poll also found that 40.2 per cent were in favour of a federal solution to the Cyprus problem and 66.8 per cent believed that a solution to the Cyprus problem was the only way out of the economic crisis. Questioned about their future intentions, 52.5 per cent of those interviewed stated that, as a direct result of the economic crisis, they were thinking of migrating. Perhaps most worrying for the future was that nearly half of that number (47.2 per cent) were young people.

That these figures remain the same was confirmed in mid-2002 by Mehmet Ali Talat, the leader of the Republican Turkish Party, who, quoted on a SIM FM radio programme, argued that the results of the municipal elections in the north of Cyprus on 30 June 2002, which saw gains for his pro-EU party, was a very visible and incontrovertible confirmation of the strengthening attitude of the Turkish Cypriot people. He said,

> our people have given a message, the message that they very much want the solution of the Cyprus problem and the accession to the EU. This, in fact, was the result of all the public opinion polls. The whole of the foreign press is concentrating on one point: that 90–95 per cent of the Turkish Cypriots support the EU. This wish, this will is an extremely serious one.

Turkish Cypriots are now acutely aware that they too could gain immensely from being part of a united Europe. They see the economic and other benefits that lie in wait for them, but they also see other effects too: freedom to travel as a recognized part of the international world once more and the right to work in other European countries; the acknowledgement of their identity and culture; the opportunity to participate in the evolution of the EU through its institutions and its projects around Europe and globally; hopefully the end to the migration of Turkish Cypriots, prompted to leave Cyprus by the lack of jobs and opportunity for themselves and their children; and, of course, the real prospect of a successful Cyprus in which they have a part and a stake.

The rapidly growing number of Turkish Cypriots who are applying for Cypriot passports at the embassies and consulates of the Republic of Cyprus around the world is evidence of the desire of the Turkish Cypriots to lift themselves out of the political impasse and make a new life in the EU for themselves and their families.

During 2000 and 2001, there was a growing public call in the northern part of Cyprus for the Turkish Cypriot leaders to engage in the debate on both membership of the EU and on a solution to the Cyprus problem. This gave significant hope that civil society amongst the Turkish Cypriots was making its voice heard and was no longer prepared to be silent. Demonstrations against the approach of the incumbent leadership were becoming a regular feature. Such a demonstration by 41 NGOs on UN Day 2001 in the north of Nicosia saw about 5000 Turkish Cypriots demanding a solution along the lines of the UN resolutions and calling for an end to nationalism and intransigence on both sides. What is more, a consistent and forceful political opposition has developed in the north of Cyprus, with political leaders taking courageous and vocal positions in opposition to those who have dominated the Turkish Cypriot political scene for the last four decades.

With support so clearly given for EU membership on both sides of the 'Green Line', the real international imperative must surely continue for the parallel processes of a solution to the problem of Cyprus and membership of the EU.

The following chapters attempt to trace and analyse how the strategy that membership of the EU could create a new dynamism in the search for a peace process in Cyprus was pursued through the European institutions. The motivation stemmed from a determined belief that the fundamental values and principles of the EU could be harnessed in support of those ordinary people on both sides of the Green Line who want nothing more than to be able to live a normal life in their homeland. It takes as its inspiration the words of the 1999 Nobel Peace Laureate John Hume of Northern Ireland, who said that 'the EU is the most successful model of conflict resolution that the world has ever known'.

3   A new world scene:

internationalizing the Cyprus conflict

The European Parliamentary elections of 15 June 1989 were never going to set the world alight. In the scale of things, June 1989 was destined to be bad timing for what, by any account, was a second-level election. The 518 members, elected by a variety of electoral procedures and systems in the then 12 Member States of the European Community, convened in their Parliament in Strasbourg, rented from and shared with the Council of Europe, on Tuesday 25 July. The turnout across Europe for the elections had been 58.5 per cent. The worrying low turnout figure led to much anguish amongst newly elected members, and much philosophizing amongst leader-writers and academics across the continent. Just what was necessary to put Europe, and in particular its Parliament, firmly in its people's consciousness, and create the sense of urgency and importance which would persuade them to come out and vote next time around?

Seen as it was amongst the European electorate as part of their nation's foreign-policy agenda, Europe, as an issue, was competing with the unprecedented and dramatic changes taking place in the world.

Regular news bulletins were dominated by the crisis in Tiananmen Square. Tens of thousands of Chinese students pursued their rally for democracy and faced up to the tanks and guns of the Red Army in Beijing's foremost plaza. On 4 June 1989, the Chinese leadership demonstrated their hardline determination to restore order and instructed its army to open fire. The deaths of many students, the closure of the universities, the arrest of some of the student leaders and the hunt for the rest absorbed page after page in the Western press. The UN and other international fora led the denunciation of China's geriatric communist leadership for its callous and murderous action against the cream of its own young people.

The soul-searching over the student deaths in Beijing was particularly poignant in Europe. Here, *glasnost* and *perestroika* were the words of the moment. Mikhail Gorbachev was loosening the Soviet strings and the countries of East and Central Europe were waking up to the real potential for change. In Germany the unthinkable was within weeks of happening – the collapse of the Berlin Wall. As the newly elected George Herbert Walker Bush settled down into the White House, the vision of the 'American dream' took on new shape. The final victory of US free-market capitalism seemed on the horizon as communist states everywhere, except a handful such as China, North Korea, Cuba and Vietnam, were in disarray or dissolution. Whilst some urged caution in this period of extreme and rapid change, the general mood was one of optimism and satisfaction, and the media hailed this as the advent of enlightened people's power.

In apartheid South Africa there were early signs of a different future as its President P.W. Botha resigned. Then, as if in response to the Tiananmen Square tragedy, the redoubtable Dalai Lama was awarded the prestigious Nobel Peace Prize, in recognition of his years of opposition to the Chinese occupation and oppression of his Tibetan homeland.

It was not surprising, then, that the elections to the European Parliament appeared as only a tiny, minor blip on any single scale of foreign-policy issues.

Similarly, the continuing division of the Mediterranean island of Cyprus since the Turkish invasion of 1974 was rarely to be seen on the agenda of international fora, governments or the media, let alone in the perception of the citizens of Europe or beyond.

But in both Europe and Cyprus a new focus was just beginning to surface. The election of George Vassiliou as President of the Republic of Cyprus in 1988 had brought to the fore a man with a different locus. Although from a family tradition of the left, and although elected with the support of AKEL, the Communist Party of Cyprus, Vassiliou was a new kind of President for Cyprus. A successful international businessman in his own right, with significant business contacts in the industrialized West, President Vassiliou set to, in a determined attempt to win over the international political arena to his cause.

At ease with the likes of Margaret Thatcher and George Bush, confident and experienced in the cultural mores of European and American business negotiations, Vassiliou engaged in a long and rigorous series of meetings around the world to internationalize the Cyprus problem. Radiating a sense of utter reasonableness and moderate good sense, George Vassiliou spent much time cultivating the moral high ground for the Greek Cypriot perspective on the continued division of Cyprus.

Whilst the reality was that the position of the Government of the Republic of Cyprus did not change, its portrayal to the rest of the world did. Over the following two years, the mood music at the international level on the Cyprus problem began, almost imperceptibly, to soften. Government leaders, leading civil servants and European bureaucrats liked and appreciated Vassiliou. Whilst the issue of Cyprus could be raised on many international stages from any of its multi-faceted angles, it remained a sensitive judgment as to just when was the right moment to elicit a positive response. However, it is true to say that Cyprus became just slightly less of a taboo subject in the following years.

In the new European Parliament, meanwhile, a drive was beginning to emerge to engage the newly elected parliamentarians in the same cause – to internationalize the Cyprus problem. A successful European election for the Labour Party in Britain saw the Cyprus issue flow into the European Parliament with renewed vigour. The election campaign had encompassed a drive to encourage the significant Cypriot community in Britain to put its votes behind the Labour Party. The necessary follow-through was that unification of Cyprus, through membership of the EU, became a tenet of the British Labour Party's foreign policy in Europe. Whilst the Labour Party hierarchy had not sanctioned this drive, and at the time in all probability did not even know it was happening, it was galvanized into support when it saw the effect on its European election fortunes. It was excited by that effect, not so much by what it meant for its numbers in the European Parliament, but what it could mean at the next general election for its majority in the House of Commons. Strategically, the seats with large numbers of Cypriot voters lay overwhelmingly within the London region – a key part of the country for Labour, given the inroads which the Conservative Party had made into the Labour strongholds in London since 1979. What is more, those same Cypriot-dominated seats were amongst the most central to the key seat strategy for the London campaign, constituencies such as Hornsey and Wood Green, Edmonton, Enfield North, Hendon and Finchley. In the final analysis, only Hornsey and Wood Green was won by Labour in 1992, whilst the other five seats, plus the unlikely one of Enfield Southgate, did actually fall to Labour in the 1997 election when the Cypriot vote came out heavily for Labour in all five. That the issue of Cyprus is key to the election success of all the incumbent MPs in those seats is evidenced by their vigorous advocacy in the House of Commons since their election of the need for a solution to the Cyprus problem.

That distinct and deliberate attempt to take hold of the Cyprus problem for the Labour Party in Europe had been well trailed during the election campaign. It was in July 1989, therefore, following the publication of the 'Food For Thought' paper by Xavier Perez de Cuellar, Secretary General of the UN, on the solution of the Cyprus problem, that a major demonstration by Cypriot women brought Labour's promise of change in Europe to the fore in the institutions of the EU.

On 19 July 1989, Greek Cypriot women began another attempt to assuage their frustration and helplessness, and to demonstrate their determination to return home, in the face of 15 long years of exclusion from a third of their homeland. As on three previous occasions, they decided to, as they put it, 'walk home'. They came together at a pre-determined spot on the Green Line in Nicosia which divides the Republic of Cyprus – free Cyprus – from what the Turkish Cypriots and Turkey call 'The Turkish Republic of Northern Cyprus', that part of the north of the island which for 15 years had been outside the control of the internationally recognized government of Cyprus. In fact just under 36 per cent of the land mass of Cyprus had since 1974 been sustained by Turkey, with a force of 35,000 regular soldiers.

The 'walk home' was to be peaceful but relentless. The women were to walk across the Green Line, which marked the ceasefire agreed on 16 August 1974, through the UN-controlled buffer zone and back to their homes in the north of Cyprus. Many of the women on the walk, on that blistering hot day in Nicosia, were themselves refugees. They had lived as refugees since 1974. In August of that year, in response to the anti-Makarios coup instigated by the military dictatorship in Greece, and with the largely silent complicity of the international community, Turkey had invaded Cyprus via the northern port of Kyrenia. It did so, it said, to protect the Turkish Cypriot population from the coup-makers. The consequences of that coup attempt were now written into the anguished faces of the women gathered on that hot July day 15 years later.

Amongst the women on that day were those who had lost close family during the conflict of the summer of 1974. Some of the women, in the fashion of the 'mothers of the missing' around the world, carried the fading photographs of members of their families who had been arrested in 1974 and had since simply disappeared. It was inevitably a highly charged and emotional crowd that moved towards the Green Line that day.

The women surged towards the Green Line, their determination and admonishments melting any hope that the young Greek Cypriot militiamen at the first line would obstruct their progress. Their numbers and the growing emotional force they generated were also too much for the UN soldiers, who were unwilling to use the significant physical force they knew would be needed to stop the tide.

The women drove forward into the abandoned church of Ayios Kassianos. The church sat smack in the centre of the buffer zone, which had been part of the no man's land in Cyprus since the ceasefire came into effect on 16 August 1974. Since that date the buffer zone had stretched snake-like across the island, encompassing the ceasefire line from coast to coast. Sometimes miles separated the Turkish lines from the Greek Cypriot. Sometimes, as in the middle of Nicosia, those lines were just metres apart, separated by a few sandbags and a UN post perched precariously between them.

As the women rested in the ruins of the church, elated by their progress and excited at being present once again in this small community church, the priests began to pray.

Whilst this was designed to be, and until that point had been, a peaceful demonstration, it was inevitable that there would be a reaction from the Turkish forces watching events from the other side of the buffer zone. There was. Armed Turkish troops, supported by Turkish Cypriot police, entered the buffer zone from the northern side. They too brushed aside the UN soldiers and began a vigorous attempt to drive the unarmed women and priests from the zone. Under the agreement that had seen the United Nations Force In Cyprus (UNFICYP) secure and control the buffer zone since 1974, it was of course true that neither the women nor the Turkish troops had a right to be there. What was clear, however, was that the incursion by a large crowd of unarmed women and a handful of priests elicited a brutal response from the armed forces of Turkey, which no doubt understood that their resolve and the legitimacy of their presence was being tested.

Beatings, screams, threats, assaults and finally the arrests of 111 women and priests resulted in the remaining crowd of women retreating back across the Green Line into government-controlled Cyprus. The world, insofar as it was interested, was to see photographs of priests being dragged to jail and unarmed women disappearing into the Turkish-controlled north, under threat of arms.

It was at the opening session of the new European Parliament in Strasbourg the following week that I made my first intervention on the Cyprus problem. That intervention underscored two things. Firstly it demonstrated to me that the new European Parliament could be used to enhance the drive to internationalize the Cyprus problem. Secondly it opened up the prospect that the Parliament offered a vehicle for pressure on the other two institutions of the EU to engage actively and seriously in finding a solution to the division of Cyprus.

For its part, the EU also had other things on its mind in the second half of 1989. The struggle to reinvigorate the European project had been hard fought. The European Single Market concept was built on introducing four freedoms: of the movement of capital, goods, services and people. Along with the four freedoms, the Single Market was posited on a streamlined and dynamic decision-making process within the institutions of the then EEC.

The Single European Act of February 1986 endorsed the concept of European law based on 'mutual recognition'. This was a fundamental change in approach, in that it institutionalized the proposal that goods manufactured in one Member State according to the prevailing laws in that country would be accepted in all others, provided those goods conformed to any high-level European standards which also existed. The 300 pieces of Single Market legislation, the brainchild of Lord Arthur Cockfield, the British Conservative appointee to the European Commission, were supposed to usher in a general set of European standards that would serve the purpose of securing safe products to underpin those national laws. Thus the first of the freedoms, the free movement of goods, could become a reality.

To secure the Single Market and drive the process along, the 12 governments agreed an operational start date of 1992. For several years '1992 – Europe Open For Business', or something similar in each language of the Community, became the slogan of the day. Along with that popular slogan and the reinvigorated ideology, it was necessary to ensure that the institutions of the Community could deliver the required legislation in time.

Until the Single European Act was secured by vote in each of the parliaments of the 12 Community Member States every single piece of legislation was taking years to go through the laborious process of adoption. One infamous piece of legislation on the harmonization of the ingredients of a jar of jam took 15 years to wend its weary way through Commission, Parliament and Council!

So, along with the concept of mutual recognition, the Single European Act introduced a truncated timescale for the adoption of legislation. The format itself owed something to the 'guillotine' procedure in the UK House of Commons by which a piece of legislation has limited time for debate before it must be presented to elected representatives for vote. This was a singular and crucial change in the balance of powers between the institutions of the Community.

The tantalizing prospect of a single European market, with all that it offered for enhanced trade, increased prosperity and popular support, through the promise of jobs and money in the pockets of the European electorate, brought the predominantly free-market governments of the European right on board for the project.

In 1989, therefore, the focus of the European institutions was inward, working against the clock to secure the 1992 deadline

for the precious Single Market. The wider international agenda im-
pinged on the institutions of the Member States as they pondered
the implications for their Europe of the increasing number of
Soviet satellite states demanding and securing limited or complete
freedom from their Soviet masters. As 1989 ended, the European
agenda was convulsed by the prospect of supporting a united
Germany, and bringing the former East Germany into full membership of the European Community as part of the enlarged Federal
Republic of Germany.

For the Council and Commission of the Community, therefore,
there was very little breathing space in an overstretched bureaucracy with an overburdened political, legislative and pragmatic
agenda.

The European Parliament, however, like all parliaments everywhere, had the capacity to chase multiple agendas. It is invariably
the nature of members of parliament that they come into office
with diverse and specific interests which elected office enables
them to drive forward in a unique way.

The Cyprus agenda was pursued actively in the Parliament.
With careful precision and timing, questions were tabled, mini-
debates initiated, comments made on the floor of the Parliament
at points of tension on the island. Resolutions were tabled on
human-rights violations on Cyprus, the tragedy of the still-missing
people, on issues of the disappearing heritage and culture of Cyprus
as well as on the political situation. Exhibitions were held in the
corridors of the Strasbourg Parliament. Influential parliamentarians,
whose views spanned the Cyprus problem, were invited to informal lunches and dinners to discuss the issues. Diplomats from both
the Republic of Cyprus and Turkey were frequent visitors to the
offices in both the Brussels and Strasbourg parliamentary buildings.

At the same time, delegations of European opinion-formers in
the European Parliament were regularly invited to London to meet
with members of both Greek Cypriot and Turkish Cypriot communities. These meetings were designed not only to discuss the
problem of Cyprus, but also to see just what aid could be given
to both communities or either, in support of their indigenous
industries in London, in particular textile-manufacturing. All in all,
the groundwork was laid to ensure that leadership on the Cyprus
agenda lay with the Labour Party in Europe.

As for the European Commission, it saw Cyprus as a third- or even fourth-level issue. Before 1989, it only needed to be addressed when it was raised tangentially in the Council, usually by Greece, in some esoteric debate about relations between Turkey and Greece or Turkey and the EU.

This changed after 1989 with the rapid disintegration of the Soviet Union. The geostrategic value of Turkey as a partner for the Western nation states, and the US in particular, was heightened. At the same time, the development of militant Islam in the Middle East initiated by Ayatollah Khomeini in Iran, and rapidly gaining adherents in surrounding states, demonstrated the value of Turkey, both as a listening and watching post and as a possible launchpad for action in the Middle East if necessary.

US policies in the eastern Mediterranean were of fundamental importance to the understanding of recent history in the region, and in developing a prognosis for the future.

During the Cold War period, the US cultivated Turkey as one of its key centres for covert activity and intelligence-gathering in respect of the Soviet Union. With the rapid disintegration of the USSR, there was initially some talk that Turkey's significance to the US would wane. The speed of events in the fortunes of Russia and the former autonomous republics was such that rather than diminishing Turkey's strategic value, that value was increased.

The emerging Islamic states of the former USSR, especially the four which had some cultural affinity with Turkey through their common Turkic-rooted languages, offered a real opportunity for Turkey to develop political and economic leadership in the region. The prospect of a strengthened regional relationship with Azerbaijan, Turkmenistan, Uzbekistan and Kazakhstan clearly fitted Turkish aspirations well, but also played to the agenda of the US as it strove to keep an open and friendly public face to the Russian Republic yet sought to keep a close, if very private, eye on it as well. The convergence of interests between Turkey and the former Soviet Islamic states may still happen. But the eastern states of the former USSR are still waiting for the economic miracle of Western capitalism. Poverty, civil war, mafia domination, the drugs trade and vice were endemic in most of these states. Whilst Turkey had already established, and continued to establish, business, cultural and deeper political links with them, the prospect of a significant beneficial political and economic relationship still remains a long-term aim.

A reinvigorated and redefined US interest in Turkey had started to develop prior to the demise of the Soviet Union, particularly when the full nature of the Islamic state in Iran began to emerge. For the US, Iran under the Shah had presented similar opportunities in the south and southwest of the Persian Gulf, as did Turkey to the north and northeast of the Balkans. The need for the US to keep more than a weather eye on its energy sources in the Caspian, Middle East and Gulf converged with its political ambitions in the region. US underpinning of the state of Israel created the constant need for reliable and focused information on the plans and projects of the Palestinian terrorist and guerrilla organizations – in particular Yasser Arafat's PLO. With Iran gone as a base for US operations, and with the Lebanon crushed as a result of a cruel and devastating civil war, the US was not quite so well equipped to keep an eye on the diverse Arab peoples as previously.

With the growth and spread of the Islamic model of Ayatollah Khomeini and the demonizing of the US that accompanied it, the need for the US to have a secure base in the region grew, and its difficulties in acquiring one grew commensurately. Attacks on US citizens, embassies and symbols of economic strength and lifestyle became commonplace across much of the Middle East. Hence, during the decade-and-a-half following the overthrow of the Shah of Iran the US explored a string of possible new and strengthened client relationships across the region. From Iraq to Israel, from Egypt to Saudi Arabia, the US worked up possible scenarios for reproducing that which had been so valuable in Iran. Some failed, in the case of Iraq quite spectacularly, but others took root.

When the shake-out of US operational activity in the eastern Mediterranean was underway, one possible venue for supporting activities into the Middle East was Turkey. Even better, sitting so close to Lebanon, Israel, Syria and Jordan was Cyprus. Cyprus under Archbishop Makarios, and also under his successors, had been less than enthusiastic about an American presence on the island. The confused political status and the military build-up on the island post-1974 offered a much more congenial prospect, and the US has established a small but important intelligence presence on Cyprus, alongside that of the British, whose surveillance facilities had been shared with it during the Cold War and on which they placed considerable value.

In the US over the preceding two decades, the Greek American lobby has pushed the US Congress into taking some significant initiatives to try and influence its own President and his administration on the Cyprus issue. The US President is obliged to make a report each six months to Congress on progress towards a solution of the Cyprus problem. This twice-yearly report, the commitment for which was extracted from the administration by a bullish Congress, has forced the President to take action in the intervening months. Over the last decade, therefore, the US administration has taken greater interest, has raised the issue repeatedly with allies – and more importantly with Turkey – and used, and continues to use, its good offices to try to broker an agreement. The administration rides a fine line between the need to retain the goodwill and allegiance of Turkey and to placate a Congress heavily influenced by the Greek-American lobby. However, when push comes to shove, the US has a clear priority which it has frequently articulated. The geostrategic importance of Turkey for US interests in the region has always proved paramount.

In common with the institutions of the EU, generally speaking, in the eyes of the US State Department the problem of the division of Cyprus was a third- or fourth-level issue. Even when Cyprus became a more significant feature in the 1990s, it did so, as far as the US was concerned, from the perspective of an obstacle that had to be cleared to allow a closer relationship between the EU and Turkey. It was this fundamentally different angle to the approach on solving the problem of Cyprus which has beset the debate between the US and the EU and its institutions, particularly the European Parliament.

This was exemplified by two visits I made as Leader of the Socialist Group in the European Parliament (in US terms the Majority Leader) to Washington and New York in November 1996 and February 1998. The visits had been organized to develop foreign-policy links with US Democrats and the Clinton administration. There had been preliminary talks about establishing closer relations with US democrats, particularly on issues of mutual concern, such as globalization and the transatlantic business dialogue, a fledgling twice-yearly e-conference to discuss specified

foreign-policy issues, with a view to developing a greater understanding of the common interests between the US and EU. Those
preliminary talks indicated that progress was on the cards. The
omens looked good.

However, at both these meetings the issue of Turkey dominated.
In the White House, with Anthony Lake, the President's National
Security Adviser, and then with Donald Bandler (subsequently US
Ambassador in Nicosia), the only issue on the table was Turkey.

In the State Department, a barrage of senior officials subjected
the European delegation to a lecture on the essential need for a
stronger relationship between Turkey and the EU. Their presentation of American strategic interests in the region was robust. But
to the notion that it was important for both Turkey and Europe
that Turkey should meet the same membership criteria that every
applicant state had to meet, they had no response.

Richard Holbrook, who was then President Bill Clinton's personal representative to Cyprus, later told me with a chuckle that
his State Department colleagues had warned him that the Socialist
Group delegation knew its stuff on Turkey.

Those delegation visits to Washington demonstrated that at
least some officials of the US administration were still struggling
to connect with the reality of the EU. Whilst intellectually com-
prehending the theory, they rationalized it as somewhere between
the North Atlantic Treaty Organization (NATO), with its Parliamentary Assembly, and their own regional trading organization,
the North American Free Trade Area (NAFTA), which at that time
brought together the US, Canada and Mexico.

That the EU really was an attempt to pool significant areas of
sovereignty across the economic, financial, social, cultural, environmental areas of activity, to name but a few, remained alien to their
thinking. That the institutions actually passed laws which took
precedence over national laws and established Europe-wide standards, seemed hard for them to grasp. That the Parliament was a
multi-national institution where the members sat in multi-national
political groups, rather than grouped behind their national flag,
was obviously a step too far.

In essence, they viewed the EU as just another international
club that, if pressed, would eventually be forced to concede to the
membership of other countries in support of American interests.

That analysis ran directly counter to the considerably more fundamentalist views of EU political leaders, who believed the European project to be a commitment that affected the very nature of Europe's democracies, the detail of the lives of Europe's citizens, their cultural and educational environment, in fact virtually all the norms and values that have affected the lives of the various European peoples for the last 100 years. For them, bringing another country into membership was not just a matter of signing up with a fanfare of trumpets and a ceremony. It was being genuinely convinced that that state, its government and people were prepared to walk the talk of European integration, pool certain national rights, and certainly not indulge in the rhetoric of nationalist extremes.

Whether by design or by default, there was also clear evidence that information about the way in which the EU worked was also skewed by misconstruction or misconception. A quite remarkable example of this was demonstrated during the discussions with Holbrook in New York. Once again the discussion was about Turkey and the way in which the EU was relating to it.

Commenting on the December 1997 Luxembourg Summit meeting of the EU prime ministers, Holbrook expressed his incredulity at the way in which, late in the night when the exhausted and fractious prime ministers were negotiating the final text of the Summit, Luxembourg – 'tiny little Luxembourg', to Richard Holbrook – had introduced a completely new demand regarding stable relations between Greece and Turkey and the settlement of disputes by legal processes, including the International Court of Justice. According to Holbrook, such a suggestion was entirely offensive to Turkey, and he expressed astonishment that the leaders of 14 Member States could be 'bounced' into such a position by the Prime Minister of the tiniest state in Europe.

I pointed out to him that his understanding was wrong. This exact formulation was certainly not new, and its genesis was clear. It had been discussed and debated fully in the European Parliament for weeks in advance of the Luxembourg Summit. I told him, 'Just as the President of the USA would temper his actions according to the mood or political will of Congress, so it was entirely right that the European Council should listen to the European Parliament'. Typically, Holbrook's response was caustic:

'Well it's even worse than I thought. It wasn't just one tiny country acting stupid, it was all 15!'

Despite all of this, it is true that the US had in latter years turned its mind seriously to a solution to the Cyprus problem. Its motivation might well have been, and almost certainly was, to aid and support Turkish ambitions to become part of the European family, but the energy, power and significance of its role needs to be harnessed in the struggle for a solution. The US has worked closely with the British Government's representative for Cyprus, Sir, now Lord, David Hannay. The US had always accepted that the UK had expertise and a long-standing relationship with Cyprus as a result of its stewardship of Cyprus during its colonial past, through to its role as a guarantor power of the sovereignty and territorial integrity of the island of Cyprus, and its extensive sovereign bases on the island, not to mention the US reliance on the information which was shared with them and came from the surveillance facilities developed by the British in Cyprus.

Correspondingly, Turkey's dependence on the US remained high. Turkish democracy was weak and subservient constitutionally to a strong military. The US influence on the Turkish military was significant. Through the supply of arms, the training of the officer cadre, the cultivation of the generals of the Turkish High Command, the divulging of appropriate information and such like, the US was able to secure a high level of support and compliance with its agenda for the region. In consequence, those of the Turkish political elite who might have wished to see their country develop into a more sophisticated European democracy, or conversely those who might have wished to secure an Islamic state in Turkey, were thwarted time after time by a strong US underpinning of the status quo.

The Turkish political elite, in an effort to secure democratic legitimacy internationally, and perhaps even to develop a bulwark against further interventions in the national political structures by its own military apparatus, began to look more seriously at the possible value of a closer relationship with the evolving European Community. This clearly worked in the wider interests of the US: firstly, by rooting Turkey in the democratic traditions of Europe, it secured Turkey against the threat of Islamic penetration from neighbouring Iran, hence guaranteeing the US a secure base in the region; secondly, it would also secure a firm ally in the heart of the European Community, whose sometimes 'fickle' partners could not always be relied upon to take a pro-American stance. Turkey's military was also in favour of closer integration with the Community. Since the days of Mustafa Kemal 'Atatürk', the generals of the High Command have been constitutionally charged with the defence of the secular Turkish state. As such they are staunchly opposed to an Islamic state model. They are also enthusiastic partners with the Western allies in NATO; hence a closer relationship with the Member States of the European Community could not but be positive, in the post-Warsaw Pact Europe.

In 1973 Turkey had opened discussion with the EEC on a customs union. The customs union was perceived as an ever-closer relationship with the European project, benefiting from a breaking down of the customs barriers between the states of the Community and Turkey. This could be expected to expedite trade and prosperity in what was in the early 1990s a burgeoning Turkish economy.

As the early years of the 1990s developed, therefore, Turkey began to push the Community for the next stages in the development of their customs union, with the declared aim of resurrecting their ambitions to join the European family. At the same time, the Community institutions and the government leaders in the European Council in particular, began to be made aware of the increasing interest of the US in securing European goodwill towards Turkey's overtures to the Member States of the EC, and to the institutions in Brussels in particular. Europe's relations with Turkey were raised to a higher plane.

4 The target for Cyprus:

joining Europe, with or without a peace agreement

In comparison to the big hitters lining up in support of a growing Turkish role and influence in Europe, Cyprus, an island in the eastern Mediterranean with a population smaller than many European cities and split by an apparently intractable 'inter-communal' conflict had very limited support in the Council of the European Community.

Of course Greece was, and remained, strong and resolute in its support for Cyprus. But in the eyes of the other European Council members, this was sometimes conceived as a disadvantage. Greece, on occasions, struggled to command support for its arguments for greater European involvement in the solution to the Cyprus problem, and for closer relations between Cyprus and the European Community. Greek leaders always had to walk a tightrope between ensuring that their commitment to Cyprus was maintained and damaging their own national interest by becoming too strident on an issue whose international sensitivities they understood only too well. Greece's protestations at European lack of interest, its reiteration of the Cyprus problem, and its search for European support for the Greek position in the various disputes with Turkey were sometimes rebuffed, almost always met with less than enthusiasm and in private discussions dismissed as part of the ongoing and tedious historical enmity between Greece and Turkey.

In the years from 1989 through the 1990s, the issue of Cyprus moved more centre stage as the European Community and, after the Maastricht Treaty of 1992, the newly named EU sought to enlarge its membership. The original hope that the enlargement of the EU could be contained to the countries of the Baltic and Central Europe was quickly dismissed. Two small Mediterranean islands, Cyprus and Malta, had applied to join the Union. Several Balkan states had either applied or indicated that they expected to apply in the near future. The membership of the Union for both Cyprus and Malta posed absolutely no problems of integration, but both had significant political problems, albeit of a different nature.

Malta was politically divided on the wisdom of membership of the European family. With a finely balanced and volatile political populace, it was clear that the people of Malta were almost evenly split on membership. During the 1990s this led to a government of the right-wing Nationalist Party submitting an application for membership of the EU in July 1990, while six years later the succeeding government of the Maltese Labour Party froze the application, only to see it reactivated when the Nationalists regained power in 1998.

Cyprus had its 'problem'. Some Member States of the EU were hesitant about introducing the fractious problem of Cyprus into the institutions of the EU, especially given the sensitivities of the issues raised between Greece and Turkey.

To add to Europe's difficulties, Turkey took strong exception to enlargement of the EU without it. It endeavoured to impose an unofficial veto preventing the EU bringing Cyprus into the fold without a common membership date for both Turkey and Cyprus. They also had strong objections to countries like Bulgaria and Romania being considered for candidate status whilst Turkey remained in a waiting room, apparently not yet ready to be declared a candidate.

At the same time, within the Council itself there was a fierce battle about the balance of power between north and south in the EU. The Southern European powers, Spain, Portugal, Greece and Italy, were worried about the enlargement to the north and east. They cited the allegiance of many of the states of the Baltic and Central Europe, to one or other of the Northern European powers.

The Southern European nations frequently found allies in France, Luxembourg and Belgium, who were desperately worried about their loss of influence on the development of Europe towards the perceived American-style free-market policies apparently being driven by the British and the Scandinavians, with Germany often a silent ally.

Whilst the Commission and the Council wrestled with diplomatic niceties to deal with these issues, the European Parliament had developed a clear view. Cyprus and Malta should become members of the EU as soon as the negotiations were completed. Turkey should be given clear guidance as to what it needed to do to achieve candidate status, and a road map should be developed with a timetable to give confidence to both sides that progress was being made.

Eventually, after long deliberation over many months, and after unofficial threats by one or other Member State not to agree to any list for enlargement unless their particular satellite was included, or their concerns abated, the European Council came to the same position as the Parliament.

Italy and Greece were reassured by the gesture to the south to include Malta and Cyprus. The granting of a significant budget for a Euro Mediterranean policy encouraged Spain and Portugal. The Nordic states were happy with the inclusion of first one and then all of the Baltic states. Luxembourg and Belgium were assured that their status as founder members of the EU would not be damaged, even if a policy for small or microstates like Cyprus and Malta had eventually to be established. Germany secured a leading-candidate status for Poland despite that country's formidable economic problems. The UK believed that the widest possible enlargement would help it to secure the change it desired, to a more flexible economic policy within the EU. Only France and the Netherlands remained out of sorts with the final agreement, and were persuaded to put their names to it only reluctantly.

Amongst the candidate countries there was general satisfaction, except for Turkey, which saw its exclusion from the candidates table as a weakening of its position regionally and politically.

The Republic of Cyprus has a long-established relationship with the EU. Since signing an Association Agreement with the EEC on 19 December 1972 it had been working towards a full customs union.

With the campaign to internationalize the problem of Cyprus launched by President Vassiliou after his election in 1988, talk of

Cyprus's ambition to apply for full membership of the European Community became increasingly open. The decision to submit the application was a sensitive political one for Vassiliou on several fronts.

Firstly, work had to be done on just what the implications would be for the Cyprus problem. Secondly, Vassiliou had to be sure that the governments of the European Community would respond positively when he made his application. Some of the European government leaders had a substantial interest in improving relations with Turkey. Would they see the application of Cyprus as simply an additional nuisance factor? The business world in several Member States of the EU was investing heavily in Turkey. How would their governments respond if forced to choose between domestic business prosperity or support for Cyprus's application to join the European Community? Thirdly, would the Turkish Cypriots react? Fourthly, the Greek Cypriot political parties were, with one exception, all in favour of membership of the family of Europe, and had been pushing the President to make the application. That one exception was AKEL, the Communist Party of Cyprus, and the very party that had supported George Vassiliou for President. The President, therefore, had to ensure that he did not risk the alienation of his major political ally before he took the step to submit the application formally.

It may have been the failure, in March 1990, of the then current round of talks brokered by the UN in New York between Vassiliou and Rauf Denktash, the Turkish Cypriot leader, to find a solution to the Cyprus problem which prompted Vassiliou to decide that he had nothing to lose by formally applying to the European Commission for membership. It may have been the collapse of those same UN talks that propelled AKEL into seeing that the only possible way to secure a breakthrough in the near future was through the European project. After all, international diplomacy had secured goodwill for the cause of a united Cyprus, government leaders were expressing support for Vassiliou, but still Rauf Denktash refused to budge. Instead he toughened his demands, and the talks ground to a halt to the unanimous and stated dismay of the UN Security Council. Where else was there to go?

So it was that on 4 July 1990, the Government of the Republic of Cyprus made its application to join the European Community.

In September of that year, the application was referred to the Commission for its 'Opinion', in accordance with Article 237 of the Treaty of Rome.

The bureaucratic procedure for membership of the EU had begun. The Opinion of the European Commission is a complex piece of work. It can take many months, and in the case of Cyprus it did! When, and only when, the Opinion is completed will the Parliament, and then the Council, give their view on whether or not an application is viable and should proceed.

The Opinion of the European Commission on the application of Cyprus for membership of the EU was published on 30 June 1993. It recognized the validity of the long-standing vocation of Cyprus to be a part of the European family:

> Cyprus's geographical position, the deep-lying bonds which, for two thousand years, have located the island at the very fount of European culture and civilization, the intensity of the European influence apparent in the values shared by the people of Cyprus and in the conduct of the cultural, political, economic and social life of its citizens, the wealth of its contacts of every kind with the Community, all these confer on Cyprus beyond all doubt, its European identity and character and confirm its vocation to belong to the Community.

The European Council meeting on 4 October 1993 endorsed the Opinion and instructed the European Commission to start work with the Government of Cyprus to help it prepare for the accession negotiations that were to follow. At the same time the Council reconfirmed that it was continuing to support the work of the UN Secretary General for a political settlement to the Cyprus question. Most importantly, the Council agreed to reassess the application of Cyprus in the light of the inter-communal discussions that were proceeding under the auspices of the UN. In particular, that reassessment would take cognizance of the positions expressed by each side, and consider the application of Cyprus to join the EU in the light of this situation.

The first stage designed to bring Cyprus within the European fold had been secured.

Behind it lay a whole backcloth of work within the institutions of the EU. In the Parliament, several initiatives had been constructed which had led to a significant, and influential, shift in the thinking and political activity of the Union.

The next piece of work pioneered by the Parliament was for the EU to have a presence at the inter-communal talks, which the UN was brokering yet again.

The UN had been the international body charged with seeking an end to the division of Cyprus ever since the 1974 trauma. The UN involvement in Cyprus was, however, of much longer standing. UNFICYP had been in Cyprus since 1964, when the UN Security Council adopted the first resolution laying down its original mandate, and at the same time appointing a UN mediator. Pre-1974, the role of UNFICYP was to prevent a recurrence of fighting, to contribute to the maintenance of law and order and a return to normal conditions. The mediator was charged with 'using his best endeavours for the purpose of promoting a peaceful solution and an agreed settlement of the problem confronting Cyprus'.

Since 1974, UNFICYP's mandate has inevitably been varied. Since then its role has been to enforce the ceasefire line, protect civilians, and assist in humanitarian aid and liaison between the two sides.

The complexity of the relationships between Britain, Greece and Turkey, the three guarantor powers of the 'maintenance of the independence, territorial integrity, security and respect for the constitution of the Republic of Cyprus', has always given a different focus to the independence of Cyprus, when contrasted with other post-colonial independence treaties. Their role, written into the original Treaty of Guarantee, accentuated a sense amongst Cypriots that their lives were 'managed' by big powers. Both the Greek Cypriot and Turkish Cypriot communities have been subject to the ebb and flow of that client and master relationship through the centuries.

It has been crucial, therefore, that in the troubled decades since 1974 those guarantor powers have generally allowed the UN to be the mediator on the Cyprus problem. It may well be that their acceptance of UN leadership has had different underlying motivations. Nevertheless, that accord has been important in ensuring that, on the whole, there has been no further major military intervention or incursion. It has also meant that when the Secretary General of the UN has identified a window of opportunity in his search for a solution to the Cyprus problem, both Greek and Turkish Cypriot political leaders have largely responded to his invitations, either immediately and voluntarily or sometimes after nudging from one or other of the guarantor powers.

However, as the Republic of Cyprus moved towards membership of the EU, the logic of the twinning of a solution to the political problem with membership of the EU demanded that the EU should be, if not a full participating party, at least an observer to the UN talks.

It was the European Parliament that once again saw that the institutions of the EU could and should be championing that cause.

If the UN was to have any potential for success in its future rounds of inter-communal talks, then it had to be sure that the proposed detail of any solution would fit with membership of the EU. Similarly, the EU had to be able to give assurance that possible interim and transitional arrangements, particularly as they related to the free movement of people across the island, could be accommodated in the membership negotiations.

I argued the position informally with colleagues in other political groups in the European Parliament, with the European Commission and even in a private discussion in Strasbourg with UN Secretary General Boutros Boutros-Ghali when he visited the city to address the plenary session of the Parliament on 14 November 1995.

The visit of Boutros-Ghali to Strasbourg was designed as part of the celebrations of the fiftieth anniversary of the UN. The Parliament wanted to ensure that it put its strong support behind the continuation and strengthening of the UN at a time of massive upheaval in the Balkans, increasing demands on the UN resources, and the pressure resulting from money due to be paid by the US. During his short visit I met with the Secretary General in his suite in the Hilton hotel. Although he was absorbed with the funding problems of the UN and his constant harrying of government leaders to bring home the promised dollars to fulfil the UN's mandates in the Balkans and Africa in particular, we found time to talk through lack of progress on the Cyprus problem and prospects for the future. Boutros-Ghali was clearly exasperated that the UN's significant efforts were getting nowhere. Wearily he claimed that 'The only card on the table at the moment was membership of the EU'. He was convinced that this could make a difference.

By the mid-1990s what had become increasingly clear was that two decades of diplomacy aimed at producing some sort of material change in the dialogue, or at least the factors underpinning the dialogue, had failed.

The application of the Republic of Cyprus for membership of the EU had created real dynamism. The desire of Turkey to join the EU, the support of the US for that bid, Turkey's pivotal role in the solution of the Cyprus problem, the implications of membership for the increasingly impoverished Turkish Cypriot community, their lack of participation in the negotiations for entry, the increasing democratic pressure on the EU states to give a definite answer to Cyprus's application, and the determination of the Government of the Republic of Cyprus, backed up by administrative and political action in support of that bid, created the friction and tension conducive to action.

Following the publication of the Commission's Opinion there was an intensive period of discussion that lasted nearly two years about just how the Union could positively influence the UN process. The EU was sure that, without any attempt to usurp the UN's role, its presence at the inter-communal talks would facilitate any proposed solution. Once the UN had accepted that principle, the discussion focused around just what sort of person should be offered the role. The EU wanted to put in a significant political figure, perhaps a former government leader or someone with foreign-policy expertise. The UN, keen to maintain its leadership role and subject to pressure from Turkey and the US, which were both arguing that a high-profile politician was inappropriate, was insistent on a bureaucrat, a professional civil servant. The latter argument prevailed, and led directly to the agreement in February 1994 between the European Council and the UN that resulted in Serge Abou, a Commission official, attending the inter-communal talks as an observer. He later presented an important report to the European Council meeting that reassessed the prospect of Cyprus's membership of the Union in line with the proposal in the Council's statement of 4 October 1993.

That reassessment took place on 6 March 1995. This was a critically important meeting for the Cyprus application. That meeting, in full knowledge of the breakdown of the last UN talks and having received the final report from Serge Abou (dated

23 January 1995) about the positions taken at those talks by both
Greek Cypriots and Turkish Cypriots, took the decision to reaffirm
the suitability of Cyprus for accession to the EU and confirmed
the will of the EU to incorporate Cyprus in the next stage of its
enlargement. It went on to make the case for membership of the
Union to bring increased security and prosperity to both communities on the island, thereby bringing about civil peace and
reconciliation. It stated categorically that negotiations with Cyprus
would begin six months after the ending of the inter-governmental
conference. The Union had set in motion a new inter-governmental
conference to make any necessary amendments to the Treaty of
Rome. This was necessary to deal with the administrative and
political problems of enlargement.

That meeting on 6 March 1995 was critical not only because it
gave a start date for the opening of membership negotiations with
the Republic of Cyprus, but because of the other clear political
deal which was struck in the Council.

It is incontestable that the members of the Council agreed
between them that there needed to be a European gesture of goodwill to Turkey. Accusations of an anti-Islamic attitude in Europe
were being raised in the Turkish media and by some politicians.
This view was given credibility when Helmut Kohl, Chancellor of
the Federal Republic of Germany, commented publicly that he
could not see Turkey being eligible to join the EU for what he
called 'cultural' reasons. There was a torrent of criticism internationally, with Turkey claiming that cultural used in this context
was a derogatory reference to specific elements of its national
faith. It was the Parliament's Socialist Group that was the first
European political party to counter the Kohl statement. I issued a
strong press statement insisting that socialists and social democrats in Europe would not support an EU that defined itself as
solely a Judeo-Christian club. The press release went on to point
out the growing diversity of the people of the EU and the strengths
which Europe derived from that diversity. Most other European
political parties overwhelmingly supported this view in the days
and weeks that followed.

At the same time as this issue was dominating the Turkish
press and making lesser, but still important, waves in some of the
European press, Turkey was arguing for the EU to grant it full

customs union. The Turkish Government saw the customs union as the next step on way to full membership of the Union. Customs union was generally perceived across the continent as a precursor to negotiations for membership, or certainly as laying the foundations for membership in the future.

So with Turkey feeling a justifiable sense of grievance by courtesy of the Chancellor of Germany, the Council meeting on 6 March 1995 was charged with reassessing the application of Cyprus to join the Union. Abou, the Union's indefatigable official on the inter-communal talks between Greek Cypriot and Turkish Cypriot community leaders, reported that a key reason for the failure of the talks was the negative attitude of the Turkish Cypriot leader Rauf Denktash. At the same time, Glafcos Clerides, then President of the Republic of Cyprus and Denktash's counterpart at the talks, had offered to demilitarize the island of Cyprus as part of the solution to the Cyprus problem. This had generated considerable political interest. Clearly on all fronts Turkish Cypriots and Turkey were on the back foot in the UN talks and in the discussions at the European Council.

With a good sense of timing, the new Minister of State at the Greek Foreign Ministry, Yannos Kranidiotis, himself Cypriot, argued for a political deal that would balance the EU's need to give a positive message to both Cyprus and Turkey. The arguments were taken forward by the Greek Foreign Minister, Theodore Pangalos, and carried the day in the Council meeting.

The statement that came from the Council meeting not only established the start date for membership negotiations with Cyprus but also made clear that the Commission would now drive forward the customs union with Turkey.

In this way the European leaders hoped to calm Turkish sensitivities by offering the coveted customs union, whilst responding positively to the Government of the Republic of Cyprus and the Greek Cypriot people.

Whilst everyone at all levels of decision-making in the institutions of the EU argued that the two decisions could not, and should not, be formally linked, it was clear that politically they had been a package. European diplomats were dispatched to Ankara to explain the decision. The Cypriot Government was clearly satisfied, even pleased with the decision concerning progress on its application for membership. What is more, progress had been made with Greece playing a sensitive and nuanced hand. Greece began to state publicly that not only had it lifted its traditional veto against the development of relations between the EU and Turkey, but that it would be the champion of Turkish entry into the EU if the necessary domestic reforms could be carried out there. It went further, and urged the EU to help and support moves for those domestic reforms.

This moment could have been, and some would argue was, if not a turning point in relations between Turkey and Greece, certainly a moment of considerable importance, laying the ground for more recent developments. It was the EU that gave Greece the political space to demonstrate that it need not always be a negative factor in Europe's relations with Turkey. The second and most significant hurdle so far to bring Cyprus into the EU had now been jumped.

For Cyprus, the next step on the way to the corridors of power in Europe was to be the actual opening of negotiations for membership. This did not materialize for 18 months more, in fact until 31 March 1998. On that date, during the British Presidency of the EU, Robin Cook, the Foreign Secretary, opened negotiations with six of the ten potential candidate countries for membership of the EU. At the conference in London, Cook hailed the opening of discussions as a major evolution of the EU and of the ending of the division of Europe, signalling the determination of all states never to see war in Europe again. He added that the Union had shown it could respond decisively and effectively to the transformation of Europe, and that the EU's efforts were being matched by Cyprus, which had made great strides on the path to accession. Cook welcomed once again the offer of the Cyprus Government to include Turkish Cypriot representatives in the team negotiating Cyprus's accession, and added that he looked forward to the day when Cyprus became a 'fellow member' of the EU.

Whilst there was a general atmosphere of optimism in the EU about enlargement, it was already being tempered by what was happening in the former states of Yugoslavia. However, this was an important moment for Cyprus. The island was included in that first list along with Poland, Hungary, the Czech Republic, Estonia and Slovenia.

But the route to that conference on 31 March 1998 had been a difficult one. During the 18 months leading up to the opening of negotiations, there had been conflicting diplomatic language, particularly from senior politicians and civil servants in some of the Member States about whether the decision that Cyprus should be part of the first group of applicant countries was really robust. In Germany and France, but particularly in the Netherlands, it seemed that the domestic talk on Cyprus was at variance with the EU talk. This had led to a constant need to reassure the Greek Cypriot population, diplomats and even some senior politicians that the country's applicant status was secure.

Over that 18 months, the institutions and office-holders of the EU were constantly being castigated by Greek Cypriots across the spectrum for the less than enthusiastic language of one or other Foreign Minister of the Union or some lesser official of a foreign ministry. Time and again they called for yet another statement confirming the decision taken on 6 March 1995. Whilst such self-doubt and the need for constant reassurance was galling to those who had worked hard to achieve the successes to date, it had its genesis in the long-standing belief of Greek and Turkish Cypriots that their fate was in the hands of others. Their worries and agitation carried a real danger, however, in that the more the demands for reassurance came, the greater risk there was of yet further inopportune comments.

As for Turkey, it began immediately publicly to refute and campaign against that part of the decision of 6 March that related to Cyprus. Turkish Government spokesmen reiterated their three consistently held arguments: that the Government of Cyprus had no right to apply on behalf of the whole island; that it could not be allowed to join the EU before Turkey itself joined; and anyway it should not be able to join before a solution to the Cyprus problem had been secured. Naturally, it accepted the part of the deal that favoured Turkey, the EU agreement to complete the customs union. It began a concerted diplomatic offensive, exercising whatever pressure it could on EU Member States' governments, either directly or through its major ally the US, to halt progress with Cyprus. This in turn further exacerbated the Greek Cypriot neurosis. The pressure was on the leaders of the European governments on the one hand not to antagonize Turkish political and public sensitivities and on the other not to back-track on the decision on Cyprus.

At the same time a serious effort was being made by the EU and its Member States' governments to engage in shuttle diplomacy between the Greek Cypriot and the Turkish Cypriot leadership. Their aim was that the EU would be the catalyst that pushed open still further the window of opportunity created by the inclusion of Cyprus in the European family and closer relations with Turkey. A host of special representatives were appointed to explore the possibility of making progress on a solution to the Cyprus problem, in partnership, of course, with the UN and in particular with Richard Holbrook, President Clinton's special representative for Cyprus.

Amongst the most prominent of the many national representatives was Lord Hannay, appointed by the British Conservative Government of John Major and reappointed in 1997 by the incoming Labour Government. Hannay, who took every opportunity to promulgate the diplomatic concept of 'constructive ambiguity', compounded the anxiety of the Greek Cypriots. His position was strengthened by the conflicting statements of officials of some Member States' governments, particularly the Dutch, French and on occasion the German, and allowed him to keep both Greek Cypriot and Turkish Cypriot leaders on their toes whilst he developed his strategy for solving the Cyprus problem.

However, the divisive nature of these political and diplomatic constructs had a cost. That cost was to expose apparent differences between the approaches of the Member States of the EU and the Union itself. These mini-schisms inevitably fed and nurtured the war of words between the regional political elites and in the media in particular. In an environment in which the Cypriot media in both communities dissect every statement made by any politician or bureaucrat who may have any possible influence on the Cyprus issue, this approach was evidently beginning to undermine confidence amongst both the Greek Cypriot and Turkish Cypriot people about the long-term prospects for both EU membership and a solution to the Cyprus problem. Eventually agreement had to be sought between the governments that all public statements on Cyprus, whether for domestic consumption or in the EU context, would be consistent with the position advocated by the prime ministers meeting in the European Council. One positive consequence of this whole debacle is that a higher level of sensitivity to the exposure of the details of delicate inter-communal discussions has evolved. If real progress is to be made it is now accepted that much of it will have to be made behind closed doors in the first instance.

But for the Government of Cyprus the opening of negotiations on 31 March 1998 brought to an end the doubt and uncertainty as to the reality of Europe's promise of opening negotiations with them six months after the ending of the inter-governmental conference. Not only had negotiations opened, but Cyprus had also been treated on an identical basis to the other states in the first group of candidates.

The third major stage in the passage of Cyprus to join the EU had now been completed.

Since that day, the European Commission has been deeply engaged in the detailed negotiations with the Government of the Republic of Cyprus over the island's membership of the EU.

Such negotiations with candidate countries are painstaking, covering all of the 80,000 pages of the so-called acquis communautaire, the body of existing legislation which any aspiring Member State of the EU must agree to adopt. The Government of the Republic of Cyprus has been rigorous in pursuing the implementation of the acquis communautaire. In a clear desire to be at the top of the queue when the next enlargement occurs, and so as not to be found wanting, the administration in Nicosia and the parliamentarians in the House of Representatives have been urged on to make the necessary and in-depth changes required to their domestic laws.

In consequence, Cyprus has been, and remains, ahead of any other applicant state in its readiness for membership of the Union. At each reporting stage, the officials of the European Commission have given Cyprus a positive and praiseworthy assessment for its commitment and its progress. For Cypriot leaders, understanding as they do the sensitivities of some European states to their political problem, the priority has always been not to be found wanting in any other way. They have sought to ensure that Cyprus was ready on every level, asking no favours, seeking maximum compliance with the acquis communautaire. The man charged with leading these negotiations for Cyprus with the EU, and for pursuing government and parliamentary colleagues to see through the changes has been George Vassiliou, the man who, as President of Cyprus, submitted the island's formal application.

As the negotiations drew to a conclusion, the big question was, what would happen next?

5 The British influence:

more than a Mediterranean listening post

At the time of the independence of Cyprus, the British negotiated a continuing provision on the island for two military bases. This agreement left some 3 per cent of the island's land mass in the control of the UK. Some of the island's main road networks cut through the bases and remain subject to the control of British authorities, including military and civilian police.

One of the sovereign base areas – Akrotiri – sits on the southern coastline between Larnaca and Paphos and is surrounded by the territory controlled by the Government of the Republic of Cyprus. Part of the other – Dhekelia – sits astride the Green Line between the government-controlled area and that controlled by the Turkish army. The Dhekelia base has long been the route for Turkish Cypriots to cross into the sovereign base area each day to work in the base or in the territory of the Republic south of the buffer zone.

The Cyprus bases have been and remain an important staging post for the British military in the region. However, the real strategic value of these military bases in the eastern Mediterranean are the little talked about but significant listening posts on the island. These surveillance facilities, which monitor missile and radar signals as well as eavesdropping on communications, have been extremely valuable to British intelligence over the years, and are much prized by the US. They returned a stream of useful information from the former Soviet Union, particularly during the height of the Cold War, when the intelligence-gathering facilities were used extensively by the Americans to monitor Soviet nuclear military developments and missile testing. More recently, the facilities have been used for surveillance of the Middle East, the Balkans and the Arab states generally, and have been enhanced by American facilities in the south of the island and the US capability supported by Turkey in the north of Cyprus as well.

Whilst public information about the role and purpose of the British posts is limited, it is clear that their geographic position was and remains of strategic importance to the UK military and intelligence services. The significance of the bases and the surveillance facilities in particular undoubtedly influences British thinking on both the solution to the Cyprus problem and the entry of Cyprus to the EU. The need for the continuing integrity of the bases could very well help to explain why the British Government has taken a clear leadership role on Cyprus vis-à-vis its partners in the EU. It is Lord Hannay, one of Britain's most experienced diplomats, who is recognized by government leaders across the EU as the key European player in the search for an acceptable, long-term solution to the Cyprus problem. It is he who engages in the shuttle diplomacy alongside the UN special representative for Cyprus, Alvaro De Soto. It is Hannay who works with both the Turkish Government in Ankara and more significantly with the US Administration and State Department as the timetable for entry to the EU and a solution to the problem run their course. For Britain, having their person as a key player in every stage of the discussions is the best way of ensuring that UK interests, both military and diplomatic, are secured. Whilst British seniority seems to have been secured for the time being, it will not have been without heart-searching for other members of the EU.

For the decades before and following the Suez crisis, the competition for influence in the region between the British and the French will undoubtedly have clouded the discussions surrounding the Cyprus problem, particularly given French sensitivities to US global power and suspicions of the special relationship between the British and the Americans. Correspondingly, any remote attempt by the French to engage in the Cyprus problem would have been expeditiously seen off by Britain to prevent even the slightest destabilization of its influence on the island.

Hence in any discussions on the future of Cyprus, be that entry to the EU or a solution to the Cyprus problem, both the UK and the US must have as a, if not the, key strategic objective the maintenance and integrity of the surveillance capability on Cyprus. By way of evidence, the facilities were the prime reason for the pressure by the Americans on the British not to abandon the sovereign bases, as had been proposed in the autumn of 1974. The security and integrity of the intelligence posts did become a real issue between the US and the UK as a direct consequence of the rift between those two countries during the Yom Kippur War in 1973. The US support for Israel had caused major schisms with its European partners in NATO, particularly the UK, whose Prime Minister, Edward Heath, had, at the height of the Yom Kippur conflict, refused to allow the Americans access to the facilities on the bases for airlift or intelligence purposes. The Americans did not easily forgive the UK Government for this breach of faith, and were determined to keep the surveillance facilities live for their intelligence services at that time. There is no reason to believe that the strategic importance of the island's surveillance capability to both the UK and the US has diminished since then.

Given the importance of the facilities to Britain, but particularly to the US, there can surely be no doubt that the other key players in the Cyprus problem, Turkey and Greece, not to mention Cypriot leaders on both sides of the Green Line, also understand their significance. The issue of the British bases must, therefore, be an important, if publicly unacknowledged, factor during any discussions on the future of Cyprus.

Therefore, whilst the US has a predominant interest in Turkey's role in the region which casts a shadow over all its dealings on Cyprus, so the British also have a significant interest in the maintenance of the British bases on Cyprus, and the role they play in camouflaging the important surveillance facilities on the island. The UK is manifestly aware of the value of the facilities in the US–UK intelligence relationship.

However, recent events in Cyprus have shown that the bases are increasingly becoming a source of irritation to local Greek Cypriots. The sometimes drunken and excessive behaviour of off-duty British soldiers has led to brawling and even murder in some of Cyprus's main tourist areas. The use of live ammunition during

British military manoeuvres in the Akamas Peninsula (earmarked as a potential national park area on the western coastline) has caused damage and destruction to an area of outstanding natural beauty, and to the breeding grounds of the endangered green and rare loggerhead turtles. This had led to a lively local environmental campaign, and protests directly to the British Government and via international ecological and political bodies. During my early years in the European Parliament, I made contact with the British Conservative Government in an attempt to persuade them to stop, or at least reduce, the impact of the British army's manoeuvres in the Akamas, but to no avail. With the election of the Labour Government in 1997, I wrote again, but this time to the incoming Labour Minister for the Armed Forces, John Spellar, urging him to deal with an issue which was a real cause for concern in Cyprus, and where he could make a difference that would certainly be noticed by Cypriots living in Britain. After agreeing to review the position, John Spellar announced that the British army would be ending the practice of using live ammunition during manoeuvres in the Akamas. Whilst a local campaign still continues to end the use of the Akamas altogether, the most damaging consequence of the manoeuvres has now been removed.

More recently, the decision of the British authorities in 2001 to erect a 100-metre-high telecommunications antenna in the area of the Salt Lake, in the British base of Akrotiri, has become another *cause célébre* which led to an attack on the base and rioting by local people worried about the environmental and health problems of such a construction.

For as long as the Cypriot population acquiesced in the presence of the British facilities, the British military and intelligence community had a vested interest in preserving the status quo on Cyprus. The bases afforded them the ability to operate their legitimate and their clandestine activities from Cyprus undisturbed, ensuring that both the British and the Americans were able to use Cyprus for wider activities in the region with less than the full glare of publicity. Although never confirmed officially, it is strongly rumoured and generally believed in Cyprus that the bases, particularly the RAF base at Akrotiri, have been the home for nuclear weapons. This was particularly damaging during the Gulf War, when the bases were used as a forward operations base rather than their normal status as a staging post, when fears were rife about the potential risk to Cyprus were it to be suspected of hosting a nuclear arsenal.

Now that the bases have from time to time caused problems with the instigation of local popular campaigns against them, British experience in other similar situations surely shows that it will probably get worse over the coming decades. Whilst public interest in the bases in Cyprus will ebb and flow, it will from time to time erupt in a display of public distrust and dislike.

Given that it is clear that the real priority for the military and intelligence services is the listening posts, it is not inconceivable that the UK could seek greater security of tenure for its surveil-lance, facilities as part of any solution to the Cyprus problem. For instance, it is worthy of consideration that the UK could perhaps negotiate away some part of the sovereign-base area in exchange for a reinforcement of the legal status of the land used for sur-veillance, which currently lies outside of the sovereign-base area. Naturally this would be developed in the context of a supportive UK gesture. For instance, the geographical positioning of the Dhekelia base between the two communities could allow the British Government to cede some small portion of the land in the base area to help with the problems of displacement of people in any realignment of territory between federated states in a new Cyprus. This could be done without jeopardizing the security or integrity of the intelligence-gathering facilities, particularly those situated outside the sovereign-base territory, for example the facilities in the Troodos Mountains and at Mount Olympus. Such a gesture could reinforce the long-term viability of the surveillance posts whilst enhancing the reputation and influence of the British in the context of their support to facilitate the reunification of a newly united Cyprus.

But such speculation is for the future. Whether or not some area of the sovereign bases is at least partially expendable is now debatable. The global 'war on terrorism' may well determine that the bases are of greater rather than lesser value to the UK and its major ally the US. The RAF base at Akrotiri offers significant possibilities for any action that may be taken to help pursue one part of George Bush's 'axis of evil' diplomacy, particularly in the context of Akrotiri's relative geographical proximity to Iraq. It is currently too early to know whether the British military and political establishment will use the Cyprus bases in any such operation, but indications are that they are giving detailed consideration to such a possibility. A senior British military officer, Lt General John Reith, the Chief of Joint Operations at the Permanent Joint Headquarters in Northwood, during a visit to the bases early in 2002 was quoted in an interview with the *Cyprus Lion* (the newspaper of the British bases in Cyprus) as saying in the context of the post-11 September 2001 situation that he was seeking ways to make the island 'more useful than it is now'. For the British Government such a contribution might be considered a relatively arm's-length way of offering support to US plans without creating major political problems in the UK, where sensitivities in the Labour Party about British involvement have grown.

However, one thing is for sure: any reshaping of the British military status on Cyprus would be controversial in Cyprus. The Cypriot economy was badly affected during the Gulf War, when the bases were used for action against Iraq. Any attempt to make such activity a normal part of the role of forces based at Akrotiri would be unlikely to receive anything other than a negative reaction from the Government in Nicosia. The bases are of course UK sovereign territory, but the British Government could surely not risk alienating the Cypriot authorities and in line with convention would seek some form of understanding from the host government. Not to do so would be a serious issue and would risk creating a significant diplomatic row. And of course the support of the Cypriot Government is very clearly important in the context of the siting of the surveillance posts. A military adventure of that sort without the acquiescence of the Cypriot Government could play badly across the range of British military interests in Cyprus. What is more, the Greek Cypriot community living around the bases has already indicated its sensitivity to the bases, and popular opposition could not be ruled out. The maintaining of sovereign bases on the island remains, therefore, a significant issue for the British Government and military in the consideration of a resolution of the Cyprus problem.

Over the last decade in particular, the British Government has been pressing the US to take an active role in seeking a solution to the problem of Cyprus. To exercise leverage in this they have worked where possible to accommodate the American agenda on Turkey. For instance, it was sometimes difficult for European politicians and bureaucrats to understand the apparently conflicting messages coming from the British Foreign Office (ostensibly with Downing Street support) that appeared to be saying 'the UK wishes to be the champion of Turkey in Europe'. To some this line of argument didn't sit comfortably with the unambiguous British support for Cyprus in the EU. The position was, of course, entirely consistent and defensible, except to those who persisted in seeing support for Turkey and Cyprus as mutually exclusive. It was, after all, in the best interests of stability and peace in the eastern Mediterranean that Turkey should be a member of the European family. All the help and support that could be given to encourage and support her vocation towards Europe should be given, notwithstanding all the difficulties in the way. However, that should not and must not have a bearing on whether or not Cyprus is welcomed into membership of the Union.

6 The London effect:

the Cypriot communities act

In the years following the 1960–74 trauma in Cyprus, the Labour Party in Britain had had an ambivalent relationship with the Cypriot community in Britain and had been cautious about, some would say almost uninterested in, the Cyprus problem.

Underlying that approach was the fact that the 1974 Turkish invasion of the north of Cyprus had occurred during a Labour administration in Britain. Britain was, of course, one of the three powers which was constitutionally responsible for the independence and sovereign integrity of Cyprus, along with Greece and Turkey.

Greek Cypriots, who are without question the dominant Cypriot community in Britain by a factor of three to one, were very aware that the Labour Government had seemingly taken no action to prevent the Turkish military strike against the north of Cyprus. They recognized and respected those Labour parliamentarians who, when the armed conflict began, called for British intervention to halt the fighting. However, the British Government's inability to influence US policy during the Cyprus crisis of 1974, and its utter lack of impact on the position taken by Henry Kissinger, US Secretary of State in particular, was seen as weakness. James Callaghan, British Foreign Secretary at the time of the invasion, is reported as confirming 'that when Wilson sent the British task force to Cyprus on 16 July, the day after the coup and four days before the invasion, the Labour Government believed that "if the American

Sixth Fleet and elements of the British Navy had put themselves between the Turkish mainland and Cyprus, the Turks could have decided to back off". But, Callaghan believed, the Americans were in no mood to take such action, and he thought it would be risking a "second Suez" to go in without them.'

Prime Minister Harold Wilson, Foreign Secretary Jim Callaghan and Defence Minister Roy Mason did receive and dine with a Turkish delegation of ministers and generals led by Turkish Prime Minister Bulent Ecevit just three days before the Turkish military actions begun on 20 July 1974. The issue of how to restore the status quo following the coup in Nicosia had been the topic for discussion at that working dinner. Harold Wilson, in his memoirs *The Final Term*, recalls that Ecevit asked him to allow a token Turkish force to use the sovereign base at Akrotiri as an entry point to launch an operation to get the coup government to capitulate; Wilson says he (Ecevit) 'received a courteous, but declaratory "no"'.

The next day, 18 July, the *New York Times* reported that the Turkish navy had moved into the waters between Turkey and Cyprus, that landing craft were being moved to Mersin and Iskenderun, that an armoured division was making its way towards the ports from its base in Adana, and that around 90,000 troops were on the move. During the night of 19 July, British forces in the eastern Mediterranean prepared to defend the sovereign bases against a possible invasion.

The UK's vacillation and lack of at least a basic strategic plan to restore stability on the island and prevent a Turkish invasion with or without the help of the US created the perception of British impotency that has been the stuff of rumour and suspicion for ordinary Greek Cypriots ever since. The strength of the rumours of British collusion has led to a magnifying of some of the resulting operational decisions: for example there is a predominant view amongst Greek Cypriots that the British had even supported the Turkish push further into Cyprus when they refused to order the strong British military presence in Cyprus to intervene and stop the fighting. Rather, it was said, the British refused to allow the Greek Cypriot forces to travel the major road networks that traverse the British bases, thereby holding them up on the way to the front line. So relations with the Labour Party for some years after 1974 were less than comfortable as far as Greek Cypriots were concerned.

Turkish Cypriots, despite being fewer in number than their Greek compatriots in Britain, have a reputation for being more predominantly Labour voters than Greek Cypriots. However, the engagement of the Turkish Cypriot community in Britain with indigenous politics had been very limited. Their voice as a community was hardly heard, and even when it was, more often than not it was assumed to be part of the more vocal mainland Turkish voice. Both Cypriot communities in Britain remain intensely involved in the politics of their homeland, and their own ethnic community politics in the UK.

There were and are parliamentarians in all parties at the Palace of Westminster who have taken and continue to take a real interest in the Cyprus problem. To say that relations with the Labour Party in Britain were sensitive for a time does not mean that some back-bench and indeed some front-bench Labour politicians did not express forthright views on the Cyprus problem and indeed on Labour's role in 1974. They became firm friends with Greek and/or Turkish Cypriots in Britain and had an undisputed reputation for their steadfastness. Foremost amongst them was Gerald Kaufman, who during his years on the back benches and more importantly during his stint as Shadow Foreign Secretary resolutely supported a solution to the Cyprus problem that encompassed the removal of the Turkish forces in return for a UN-led constitutional settlement.

Similarly, there were Conservative politicians in Europe who took a similar interest. Sir James Scott Hopkins, the Conservative Member of the European Parliament for the Forest of Dean, chaired the European Parliament–Cyprus House of Representatives Parliamentary Delegation for many years. Coming from a military and intelligence background, he had more than a passing professional interest in Cyprus, and ensured that he kept fully involved with those Labour members in the European Parliament who had an interest in the Cyprus cause.

In general, the cause of Cyprus continued to be heard from time to time from both the Greek Cypriot and Turkish Cypriot perspective in the House of Commons. But, once again, the cause of Cyprus was championed not by government but by parliamentarians with a vested constituency interest or genuine concerns for justice, democracy and freedom, or both. Occasional though it was, the Cyprus political debate in Britain was probably greater than that in any other European country, with the exception of Greece, although probably slightly less so than in the US Congress.

By 1989, the sense of frustration and helplessness amongst the Greek Cypriot community in London was almost palpable. The Conservative Government of Margaret Thatcher had done very little to champion a solution to the Cyprus problem. British ministers did not visit the island, they did not choose to use the international fora to any great extent to pursue a solution for Cyprus, and although some local MPs supported the urgent need for a solution, the Conservative Party in Parliament was not engaged. On the emerging issue of Cyprus and its relationship with the EU, the Conservatives had a clear view. Whilst they supported Cyprus within the EU, that could only happen in the context of a resolution of the Cyprus problem. Some of their local MPs with heavy Greek Cypriot constituencies tried to nuance that political position, but their various foreign ministers over the years let them down time after time with their clarity in public.

It was in this environment that the European elections of 1989 took place. In my own constituency of North London, which was heavily influenced by the Greek Cypriot vote, I argued strongly that Cyprus in the EU could provide a new basis for beginning to seek a solution to the Cyprus problem.

News about the evolution of Labour Party thinking on Cyprus and the EU spread rapidly throughout the Cypriot community, particularly the Greek Cypriots. Europe was a vehicle that the Cypriots in Britain had not really started to consider in any organized way until this moment. The prospect of having a source of political influence outside of the sterile debate in the UK held great appeal. The threads of the European vision also held a message for Cyprus.

So it was that the Labour Party became associated with the development of the policy for Cyprus in the EU as a means of securing a solution to the problem. However, having articulated this argument and subsequently won the European election – doing well particularly amongst Greek Cypriots on that argument – was not enough. There was now an absolute need to root that policy initiative firmly in the Labour Party policy agenda. I was not prepared to be caught in the trap between members of the

European Parliament, who had secured the confidence of the Cypriots in Britain on a well-defined policy, and the policy-makers in the Party, who could at any time countermand that approach. Labour MEPs were not to be the victims of the same dissonance with their party hierarchy that had done such damage to Conservative MPs on the issue of Cyprus.

So began a campaign to entrench the initiative in Labour's policy agenda, which stretched through until the European election in 1994, by which time those of us involved believed we had succeeded. After 1994 the campaign became one of ensuring that the Labour Party maintained that position so that once it won government it could take steps to move the policy forward, and carry out its commitment to Cyprus by support for its membership of the EU. Both amongst Labour colleagues in Europe and within the Labour Party itself at a grass roots and national level that position was made immeasurably easier by my election as a British Labour politician to the most significant political post in the European Parliament from 1994 to 1999, that of Leader of the largest group in the Parliament, the Socialist Group. That post gave me a position of authority on European issues during the following three years, in which the Labour Party remained in opposition in Britain, and unique access to government leaders, the European Commission and the Council.

During these three years to May 1997, I became a regular member of the caucus of socialist/social-democratic prime ministers meeting in the European context. In 1994, this group had consisted of just four government leaders. By 1997 it was eight, and within weeks of the British general election in 1997 that caucus group of prime ministers had become the majority group in the European Council as the French and then the German elections swelled the number of socialist/social-democratic governments to 11 of the 15 Member States of the EU.

But in the first instance, in 1989, a great deal of work needed to be done to open up the debate on Cyprus within the British Labour Party. Much of this hinged on the impact of both Cypriot communities on local Labour Party activity. In the pockets of Cypriot population across Britain, meetings were held, the message of Cyprus in the EU articulated and advice given on how members of both communities could influence their local MPs at

Westminster. Local constituencies were encouraged to raise the issue by submitting resolutions to Labour's annual conference. Exhibitions were held and the Party's foremost spokespersons invited to speak to large and enthusiastic Cypriot audiences. Leading politicians from both communities in Cyprus were invited to Britain to speak with Labour politicians.

The Greek Cypriot community was first to engage with Labour under its own steam. Prominent members of that community, having made use of the opportunities to make contact with the party, were soon to be seen at events up and down the country talking to and engaging Labour's policy advisers and politicians.

In the meantime, visits were arranged for a Greek Cypriot delegation to travel to Brussels and speak to influential parliamentarians and plans set in train for the first of two similar visits for a Turkish Cypriot delegation to follow.

Why did the Labour Party hierarchy and party machinery agree to engage in what was, in the first instance, the particular campaign of a single parliamentarian? Firstly, the old adage, nothing succeeds like success. Here was an issue that had brought a significant number of votes to Labour in a marginal European seat which contained potentially six seats in the House of Commons – and that had happened in just one London European seat with approximately 120,000 Cypriot voters. Something like a quarter of a million Cypriots lived across London. Not only was it a matter of votes: the Cypriots were very well organized in their own communities and brought significant amounts of structural and campaign support. Secondly, it happened on the back of the development of an issue that provided an important distinction in policy between Labour and Conservative Parties. Thirdly, if this issue could swing votes in some numbers in a second-level election like that to the European Parliament, then it must have the potential to swing a significant number of marginal seats – particularly in London, the home of most of the Cypriot community, both Greek and Turkish – in the forthcoming general election. London was a key strategic region for any election to the Westminster Parliament in the general elections of the 1980s and 1990s. That strategy was vindicated when the six targeted Cypriot-dominated seats in three boroughs in north London were all won in 1997 and held again in 2001. Lastly, the issue of Cyprus, its division and continuing problem was reawakened in policy terms in the Labour Party, and many more Labour MPs and candidates became involved and committed.

The British Conservatives in the European Parliament were very late to read the signs and see what was happening. They relied on their doyen of the Cyprus problem in the Parliament, Lord Nicholas Bethell. Bethell, as a member of the House of Lords as well as a north London member of the European Parliament, had for some time chaired the all-party Friends of Cyprus group in Westminster. This, it was assumed, meant that Conservative interests on Cyprus in both Westminster and Europe, and consequently the Cypriot vote in the UK, was reasonably secure. Bethell was, however, more active on Cyprus in Westminster than in Brussels, leaving the major Conservative role in the European Parliament to his colleague, Sir James Scott-Hopkins. Bethell would speak in the occasional major debate, but was not involved in lower-level issues that tended to absorb the Cypriot community in London and indeed Cypriots in Cyprus. He certainly did not engage in the round of activity that opened up after the June 1989 elections and stretched right through until the next European election in 1994.

Throughout that time a coalition of members of the European Parliament interested in a solution to the problem of Cyprus was being established that was cross-nationality and cross-party. In particular, a grouping of the libertarian left – Social Democrats, Greens, Radicals and Liberal Democrats – were making common cause, and drawing into their ambit interested individuals in the other parliamentary groups.

So by the time of the European election in 1994, the issue was established in the Labour Party's policy rhetoric. It was anyway a strength of Gerald Kaufman's policy portfolio. As Shadow Foreign Secretary he had the great advantage of knowing the underlying issues, had visited Cyprus and was an advocate of a UN-brokered solution. He readily understood and endorsed the policy of Cyprus in Europe without difficulty. His successor, Jack Cunningham, although not as proactive on the issue, was passively supportive and never failed to speak to the case when asked.

It was Jack Cunningham's successor, Robin Cook, who really brought the issue to life in Westminster and played it to Labour's advantage. In advance of the 1997 general election, north London was a regular stopping-place for Robin Cook, who visited several times. Together with the north London Labour candidates, I arranged for the Shadow Foreign Secretary to speak at a meeting with an audience of mainly, although not exclusively, Greek Cypriots. Two weeks later he returned to speak to a mainly, although not exclusively, Turkish Cypriot audience with the Turkish Cypriot opposition leader Mustafa Akinci, who had just completed a detailed programme I had organized for him in Brussels.

At both meetings, Cook was precise, clear and cogent. He argued the need for a solution to the Cyprus problem. He made clear that Britain under Labour would actively pursue the UN-brokered talks. His grasp of the issues was evident. He made clear that the Turkish Cypriot community must be given clear guarantees of its security, but that the threat of force by Turkey must end. He concluded by arguing that Cyprus's membership of the EU offered a layer of support and guarantees that had not been available previously and should be welcomed as a contribution to the solution. But he argued that no country should expect to have a veto over the membership of the EU by any other applicant state. Labour was committed to Cyprus in the EU, preferably as one united country, but if that was not to be then as it currently existed on accession.

For us in Europe, there was only one thing left to do, and that was to ensure that the Labour Party in government carried out that commitment.

Once again it was Robin Cook who, true to the words he had uttered at the pre-election meetings, saw through Labour's commitment to Cyprus. As a member of the General Affairs Council of the EU, he argued consistently for membership of the Union for Cyprus. At the end of March 1998, as President in Office of the EU during the British presidency of the EU, he officially opened negotiations with Cyprus and five of the other candidate states for membership. This initial tranche of six candidate countries was later extended to ten.

The campaign for party endorsement of the policy initiative that had been launched in advance of the 1989 European election campaign had been won.

During his stewardship of the British Foreign Office, the succeeding Secretary of State for Foreign Affairs, Jack Straw, staunchly

maintained the clear positioning established by Cook in the previous four years.

Before leaving the issue of the British Labour Party and the
cause of Cyprus, there is one further element of the relationship
that needs to be explored. That is the role that the Greek and
Turkish Cypriot communities play within the grass-roots structures
of the Labour Party. By 1989, the Greek Cypriot community was
already well established within the Labour Party. Many were
members of the party. There was a growing number of Greek Cypriot
local authority councillors, particularly in London. Some of them
had already been elected to the most prestigious office in a local
authority, that of Mayor. Since 1989 that number has grown considerably as the ability to exert influence and make a difference
became more evident.

The Greek Cypriot community throughout Britain was well
organized. It had a network of organizations based on a range of
factors from their village origins in Cyprus, to business, cultural
activities, language classes for children and community centres.
It met regularly in a host of fora, communicated well between
networks and, all in all, was a sophisticated and articulate community integrated and at ease in British society. Many of the
second- and third-generation Greek Cypriots are assuming important roles in the UK establishment at senior levels of academia,
business and the professions. They did not have a Greek Cypriot
member of parliament. This became the focus of activity for several of the more prominent younger Cypriots active in the Labour
Party, and there was no doubt that before long one would emerge.

In 1989, the Turkish Cypriot community was much less evident in the grass roots of the Labour Party. It had fewer members
of the party, with a smaller number of elected local-authority
councillors. In terms of community networks, it had a much
more sporadic communications structure, usually confined to the
Turkish-language newspapers for the wider community with a
restricted number of active community leaders in regular touch
with each other.

By 1989, Turkish Cypriots had left, or were leaving, their
homeland in their thousands. At that time, with the considerable
support of mainland Turkey, there was a reasonable economic
situation in the north of the island, but even so Turkish Cypriots'

general perception was of stagnating opportunity, with no prospect of the situation improving.

They were also becoming increasingly concerned about what they described as 'becoming a minority in their part of the island'. This referred to the accelerating official policy in the north of the island of bringing mainland Turkish 'settlers', providing them with jobs and settling them in homes or farms previously owned by Greek Cypriots who had fled in 1974, or indeed the homes of Turkish Cypriots who had emigrated. The number of settlers had grown considerably, and continued to grow throughout the decade of the 1990s. The sense that many of these people (largely peasant farming families from Anatolia) had no empathy with the pre-vailing culture in the north of Cyprus exacerbated the desire of the indigenous Turkish Cypriots to leave.

There was also a large and dominant Turkish influence in the north. The presence of 35,000 Turkish troops amongst a popu-lation that was estimated at 120,000 in August 1974 was a clear and visible daily sign of just where decisions were made and influence exercised. The reliance of the north of Cyprus on Turkish funding for its existence further demonstrated that dominance.

Emigration amongst the Turkish Cypriots began in substantial numbers after the inter-communal strife in 1963–64, but since 1974 tens of thousands of Turkish Cypriots emigrated to the UK, Australia and North America, among other places. With the advantage of having been taught English, and being familiar with the British legal and administrative structures as a result of the legacy of Cyprus's colonial history, the English-speaking countries were an attractive destination. In 2001, according to Turkish Cypriot politicians, and as published in the Turkish Cypriot press, some 115,000 mainland Turkish settlers were living in the north of Cyprus. Indigenous Turkish Cypriots were estimated to be only about 88,000.

Within the territory of the EU, the single largest community of Turkish Cypriots live within the UK, and largely within London. It is an interesting sociological fact that, despite the tensions and difficulties in Cyprus, the Turkish Cypriot and Greek Cypriot émigrés settled in the same parts of London and were generally observed to be following identical patterns of settlement as they became more established and prosperous. Later waves of

Turkish-speaking émigrés have also tended to settle around the established Turkish Cypriot community, attracted by the local community provision for the Turkish language, culture, media, education and support services. These more recent waves of Turkish Kurds and other mainland Turks have become substantially larger in number than the Turkish Cypriot community. This inevitably created a difficulty for the articulation of a distinct Turkish Cypriot voice.

Turkish Cypriots initially came to Britain with full rights as citizens of the British Commonwealth. This ensured that they were able to work, live and integrate fairly quickly into British life. In the past, they were, generally, not required to live with the indignities of life as refugees or asylum-seekers in the UK, to which many of the other Turkish-speaking communities were subjected. This situation changed in the late 1990s, and new immigrants from the north of Cyprus were required to secure a visa in advance of entry to the UK. This resulted from the tightening of British regulations following the identification of a growing problem with the use of the north of Cyprus as an entry route to the UK for mainland Turkish émigrés.

The result of the complex concentration of Turkish-language immigrants over the last five or six decades was that, in contrast to the newer arrivals, the more mature Turkish Cypriot community was established in Britain, many of its members owning their own homes and businesses. They and succeeding generations were active in the commercial and trading life of Britain, and were breaking through into the professions as well. However, they did not command the same political or media attention as some of the larger, more recent and deprived refugee or asylum Turkish communities did.

The Greek Cypriots were always many more in number in the UK than the Turkish Cypriots. They also played a more influential role in ethnic community politics generally. This was largely because there was no mainland Greek community of any significant size or concentration in the UK and, as a consequence, the Greek Cypriots constitute by far and away the largest part of the Greek-speaking part of British society. They have, therefore, always been represented at a political and community level as part of the UK minority scene.

For some years, however, the Turkish Cypriot community had been categorized with all other Turkish-speaking or Turkish people in the UK. It was the more sophisticated, better-educated Turkish Cypriots who performed many of the essential support services for the secondary waves of immigrants from mainland Turkey. They were particularly effective in counselling, language services and interpretation, advice surgeries and the like. Largely because much of the time and energy of the active members of the community was expended on important voluntary work and effort of this type, the community did not establish the same level of political contacts and profile amongst UK-based politicians or government tiers at local, regional or national level as their Greek Cypriot counterparts.

Once again it was the emergence of Europe as an issue which galvanized the Turkish Cypriot community to raise their expectations of the British political process and to exert pressure on the political parties and structures in the north of Cyprus.

Together with Labour members of the House of Commons, I opened up the debate with the Turkish Cypriot community on the benefits for Cyprus and Cypriots of membership of the EU. In a process similar to that undertaken with the Greek Cypriots, meetings were arranged in London for European members of the European Parliament. For those MEPs it represented their first opportunity to meet and talk with Turkish Cypriots. A German MEP, Mechtild Rothe, who chaired the European end of the Joint Parliamentary Committee between the European Parliament and the House of Representatives of the Republic of Cyprus, came to London to talk with both Turkish and Greek Cypriots.

For MEPs, these two London-based communities represented a rich source of information, and also provided a forum for the testing of ideas and approaches to the Cyprus problem. Most European MEPs had never travelled to Cyprus, and if they had it was to meet with parliamentarians from the House of Representatives who were, of course, all Greek Cypriots. So London became a useful opportunity to hear the views of Turkish Cypriots. The Dutch Liberal MEP, Jan Wilhelm Bertens, who was charged by the Parliament with drawing up its report on the application of Cyprus to join the EU, also visited London for such talks. Another unique feature of those communities was that they were already resident in the EU. Therefore they had a real feel for the potential impact of the EU on Cyprus from the perspective of citizens or residents already on the inside. Those MEPs and European Commission officials who visited the two Cypriot communities in London were astonished to find that the Greek and Turkish Cypriots worked and lived side by side without obvious rancour or undue conflict. Cypriot traders worked side by side in street after street in certain parts of London; they worked together in business relationships and associations. The European visitors paid calls on the Haringey Cypriot Centre, an unusual experience, as it was a centre provided by the local authority for all Cypriots. It was also unique in having an elected Turkish Cypriot chairperson and Greek Cypriot manager.

The success of those meetings led the European members of the Joint Parliamentary Committee to issue an invitation on two separate occasions for representatives of the Turkish Cypriot community in London to make presentations to all of its European members. In accepting, the Turkish Cypriot leaders in London gained a unique experience that gave them a significant profile in their own community in London, but more importantly reflected back into the north of Cyprus. Whilst the Turkish Cypriot leadership on the island was refusing to engage in discussions or negotiations and had, in effect, cut off relations with EU diplomats and officials, a group of community leaders from London had taken the voice of Turkish Cypriots right to the heart of the EU in Brussels – courtesy of the office of the Leader of the Socialist Group in the European Parliament.

Those meetings had consequences for both the community in London and in the north of Cyprus. In London, a diverse group of Turkish Cypriot organizations established an umbrella organization called the Turkish Cypriot Forum for Europe. This organization, together with the Cyprus Turkish Democratic Association, went on to produce an annual declaration of support for the vocation of Cyprus and its people to be part of the EU. What was so different about this organization was that it printed its declaration in a single document in English, Turkish and Greek bearing the flags of the Republic of Cyprus, Turkey and Greece. Each year the declaration was launched at a reception in the middle of London and was attended by politicians of all political parties and from the various

tiers of government in Britain. This was the measure of the evolution of Turkish Cypriot representation in the political processes
in Britain over just a handful of years.

In the north of Cyprus, the activities of the community leaders
in London were causing consternation. The visits of the London-
based community leaders to Brussels were covered extensively in
the news in the north of Cyprus, as were the visits of the assorted
Europeans to London. Those activities began to generate a much
more intense debate on the importance and value of the EU itself,
and its potential as a vehicle for change.

Having reflected on the considerable impact of the meetings
between the Turkish Cypriots and MEPs in both London and
Brussels, I invited the two principal opposition leaders in the
north of Cyprus to visit Brussels. Mustafa Akinci, leader of the
Turkish Communal Liberation Party and Mehmet Ali Talat, leader
of the Turkish Republican Party, subsequently followed a comprehensive programme of contacts.

I wanted to do two things with these visits: firstly to give an
international platform to the two major Turkish Cypriot opposition
leaders; secondly to ensure that those in positions of power and
influence in Brussels, both in the Parliament and the Commission,
were made aware that there was a diversity of views amongst the
political leaders in the north of Cyprus. That such a political
diversity existed amongst the Turkish Cypriot political elite was
not generally understood in the wider world. The isolation of the
Turkish Cypriots since 1974 had meant that the political opposition in the north of Cyprus had found it virtually impossible to
secure an international platform outside Cyprus and Turkey. In
consequence, knowledge of the credentials and the views of the
two politicians who represented a large, arguably the largest, section of Turkish Cypriot views, were scarce. The two visits generated
much interest from political figures at the top of the European
Commission to back-bench MEPs, and certainly within the north
of Cyprus itself, where press interest was immense. The tactic to
engage Turkish Cypriots directly in the discussion on Europe had
succeeded. But this time there had been a secondary tactic, which
was to engage the European side in a real learning experience as well.

Both Akinci and Talat have been powerful advocates of an
alternative approach from that of the dominant leadership in the

north of Cyprus. Their arguments were very largely reflected in the community in London where the wider debate had begun. Whilst holding robust views on the various aspects of a solution to the Cyprus problem, they were refreshing in that they did believe fundamentally that a negotiated settlement could be reached with the Greek Cypriots. They wanted the Turkish Cypriot side to show the political will to engage more positively in those negotiations. It was no surprise that Talat went on to be a leading voice of legitimate political opposition in the north of Cyprus.

In a further effort to carry out the exhortation of the European Council and spread news and information to Turkish Cypriots about the process of European integration, there was a further important initiative in London. Acknowledging the importance of the London Turkish Cypriot community in kick-starting and influencing the debate in the north of Cyprus, a meeting was organized in January 1998 specifically to outline progress on the detail of negotiations for the entry of Cyprus to the EU.

Working through the established organizations in both communities, I invited 100 leading Greek Cypriots and 100 leading Turkish Cypriots to a meeting to be addressed by George Vassiliou, the chief negotiator with the EU for the Government of the Republic of Cyprus, and Dr Leopold Maurer, the European Commission's Head of the Enlargement Task Force responsible for Cyprus. The meeting was billed as specifically excluding talk of the Cyprus problem and as being the opportunity to inform Cypriot citizens living within the EU about the process for the entry of their homeland. The meeting caused a tumult of debate within the Turkish Cypriot community in both London and Cyprus. Extreme nationalists argued that no Turkish Cypriot should attend the meeting, whilst the Turkish Cypriot Forum for Europe argued the opposite. Hours of time were devoted to it, and in a two-hour phone-in on the local Turkish radio station in London political leaders phoned directly into the live radio debate from the north of Cyprus, encouraging the invitees either to attend or not to attend, depending on their position.

On the day of the meeting, police were required to hold back a small but vocal demonstration of extremists, identified as mainly Turkish rather than Turkish Cypriot, who sought not only to abuse those attending but also to put strong pressure on those Turkish

Cypriots who arrived to turn back. Despite such pressure, the great majority of the invitees attended, and the questions and comments were dominated by the Turkish Cypriots present.

Through all of these years the involvement of the Turkish Cypriot community in London was a critical element in ensuring that MEPs were kept abreast of the mood and motivation of their community in the north of Cyprus. Both communities in London were closely involved with their homeland. Contacts were regular, and visits were frequent. Political leaders from both Greek and Turkish Cypriot political parties paid frequent visits to their respective compatriots in London, in recognition of the impact and influence they could exercise in British political circles and on opinion back home. In that respect, the Turkish Cypriot community has exercised a pivotal role on the evolution of the political and media debate with regard to membership of the EU in the north of Cyprus. The fact that a poll conducted by the London-based Turkish Cypriot newspaper *Toplum Postasi* showed that among Turkish Cypriots living in the north of Cyprus something like 97 per cent expressed an opinion in favour of membership of the Union owed much to the pioneering work of the London community.

Some of the leaders of the London community had also taken significant personal risks in their positioning with regard to the EU. There was no doubt that they had exercised real leadership and had been subject to considerable pressure as a result. To their immense credit, they had a tremendous impact.

7 The Greek dimension:

after the 'earthquake dialogue'

One of the acknowledged regional weaknesses of recent decades in the eastern Mediterranean has been the absence of a commitment to consensus-building amongst the leading political players. Leadership when it has come has often been confrontational or chauvinistic, and there has been much reliance on the big powers to intervene to restore calm and caution. It has taken the major trauma of first one and then two devastating earthquakes to bring to the fore an initiative from within the region itself. Whilst all the participants realize that the dialogue which begun after the Turkish and then Greek earthquakes is a long game, the fact that it exists is a cause for hope. But the signs of a changing climate began to emerge before the earthquakes, and can be traced back to the evolution of a new political style in Greece which has elicited at least some response from within the Turkish political elite.

Whilst from Turkey's perspective Greek motives would have been questionable, Greece played an adept hand in resolving the impasse in relations with Turkey, leading to progress on the application of Cyprus at the important meeting of the General Affairs Council on 6 March 1995.

In some respects it may mark the point in the last decade of the twentieth century in which the Government of Greece really began to play to its strengths in the European Council. From it flowed a new approach to regional and European politics that developed into a sustained, quiet, long-term strategy. What was important was that for the first time in some decades there was a real attempt to exercise some leadership from within the region, on issues and conflicts that had for a long time been considered outside the control of regional players.

The history of Greece in the last quarter of the twentieth century is interesting. The collapse of the US-supported dictatorship of the Greek colonels in 1974 ushered in a period of national rebuilding. The period of the junta had been painful in the extreme. The active support of the US for the dictatorship of the Greek colonels left an abiding mistrust of the US role and interests in the region that continued to cloud the perspective of a whole generation. To many, the current US advocacy of Turkey and its clarity about Turkey's geostrategic importance to the US reinforced mistrust and suspicion of American motives towards Greece and the region more generally.

The period that followed the collapse of the junta saw Greece turn to the EU for the underpinning of its democratic roots. The EU adopted a high-risk strategy with regard to Greece, and then also to Spain and Portugal. As all three countries emerged out of dictatorship, the EU was confronted with a quandary. Should it seek to bring each country into the EU rapidly, as they themselves desired, despite the challenge that fledgling and still inherently unstable democracies could present to the EU itself? Or should it take it more slowly, support the development of a market economy and participatory democracy, whilst waiting until each country had seen through the early stages of national regeneration?

In each case the EU decided for rapid integration.

That decision is often held up by the present applicant countries as establishing a precedent that should be followed in their case. But whilst seductive, the argument once again ignores the massive changes which have occurred in the EU since the earlier decisions. Any country seeking to join the EU now is not just joining a rather fusty, bureaucratic and ponderous organization. Whilst it is true that the EU still retains more than a slight element of each of these behavioural tendencies, it is now the EU of the Single Market and the single currency. It now has a political presence in the world that the leaders of the EEC in 1974 had not even begun to imagine. The collapse of the Soviet Union has also propelled the EU into a significantly enhanced role in the economic and democratic architecture of the world.

Greece, however, has some unique attributes, both geographical and cultural, when compared to other EU states, that account for some of its apparently awkward positioning on some issues. The Greek language was a distinguishing feature, given its distinct difference from the spoken and more particularly the written scripts of its European allies. On joining the EU it became the Union's southeastern border. It remains the only EU Member State that has no land border with another EU country, bounded to the south and west by the Mediterranean, to the east by the Aegean Sea, with its potential for disputes with Turkey over the ownership of certain islands, with mainland Turkey itself sitting immediately beyond the Aegean. To the north sits the chaos of Albania, the remaining Yugoslav states Serbia and Montenegro, and the former Yugoslav states Bosnia and Macedonia.

The Greek people share a strong religious link to the Christian peoples of the former Yugoslavia through the Orthodox Church. The Church exercised a significant force on the lives of Greeks. Although that trend was lessening, there is no doubt that the influence of the Church was more pervasive and deep-rooted than in most of the other Member States of the Union. Whether in Greece, Serbia or Russia, the Orthodox Church has a strong nationalistic element to its ideology. Whilst at some points in its history this has been a useful construct for Greek leaders, it has also created some considerable difficulties for the political leadership of Greece, for instance in the run-up to and during the Bosnian war in particular. On any objective assessment of the situation, the Greek Government exercised considerable leadership in maintaining tacit support for the NATO actions and consequent political evolution in Kosovo, and Serbia more generally, despite strong internal division and dissent.

The sensitivities of recent Greek history combined with its geographical isolation from the rest of the EU, and given its religious and cultural affinities created a volatile and fragmented political environment that had to be handled with care. During the necessary nation-building period of the post-junta years, however, the Greek political leadership had other priorities and was not able, or in some instances willing, to pursue some of the modernization which Greece needed if it was to prepare for the rapidly emerging high-technology economy.

The death of Andreas Papandreou, the veteran Greek Prime Minister, in 1996 marked the end of an era in Greece. The election of Costas Simitis as Prime Minister of Greece put in place a man quietly determined to pursue modernization and reform. Aware of the size of the problem, the need for urgent domestic economic and social reforms, the need to demonstrate a willingness to deal with the most difficult issues both at home and with the country's neighbours, and perhaps most importantly the need to change the perception of Greece in the international arena, Prime Minister Simitis presented an absolute break with the past.

During the first two years of his leadership of PASOK, the Pan-Hellenic Socialist Movement, there was a defining struggle for leadership between his new tendency and the traditionalists. Perhaps against the odds in a country where emotion has a strong influence on politics, the more technocratic 'new' tendency won and Simitis was confirmed as leader and Prime Minister.

A good example of the determination of the new-style Greek leadership was quickly evident. Greece's exclusion from the first group of countries into 'Euroland' (membership of the EU's single currency) gave the new Greek leadership a focus around which to galvanize national pride and effort. The consequent remarkable changes that were carried out in the drive to become a member of the single currency were striking and noteworthy. In May 1998, at the launch of the single currency in Brussels, 11 of the 15 Member States of the EU were assessed as having met the criteria for membership of the Euro, as laid down in the Maastricht Treaty. Of the four outside the club, the UK and Denmark were not assessed as they had both made the political choice and secured the necessary treaty exemptions to stay outside. Greece and Sweden were both assessed and held not to qualify.

The 11 Member States who originally made up Euroland went to great lengths to demonstrate the way in which their economies had been driven closer together on a range of indicators in preparation for the single currency. However, even at that early stage the really striking performer was the Greek economy. On the same indicators it was showing dramatic moves towards the necessary criteria for membership. Such was the progress over the

following months that Greece was invited to join Euroland on
1 January 2001.

But it had not just been in economic policy that the Simitis
Government had created waves. At European Council level his
quiet and almost deliberately understated approach had earned
him a respect and understanding amongst his peers, particularly
as he had sought to be constructive, if firm, with regard to the
EU's relations with Turkey, and as he held the line with the NATO
allies during the Bosnian and Kosovo wars.

Furthermore, Simitis had pursued a policy of dialogue with
Turkey. His appointment of George Papandreou as Foreign Minister
of Greece was a bold and inspired move, giving rein to a man
who, perhaps as no other Greek politician, had the potential to
make a major impact on the strategic shape of the region, and
in particular to change the nature of the relationship between
Greece and Turkey.

With Papandreou, Greece had in its Foreign Ministry a man
with indisputable links and respect in the US. Son of Andreas
Papandreou, he had spent much of his youth and been educated
largely in the US. In the delicate work of shifting Greek opinion
in relation to Turkey, the confidence of the US State Department
was critical. Papandreou was perfect for that role, by background,
education, career development, contacts, manner, style and vision.

The appointment of Yannos Kranidiotis as Minister for European
Affairs was a second and important appointment. In Kranidiotis,
Greece had a man who knew the institutions of the EU inside
out and had many contacts with them. Kranidiotis had been a
member of the European Parliament and had also been partly
responsible for the foreign relations of PASOK. In that capacity, he
had made links with a host of senior European politicians. The
close interlinking of Greek work on the international agenda with
both the US and Europe would be a vital strength for Simitis. The
untimely death of Kranidiotis in September 1999 could have
caused major dislocation on that front, but with the subsequent
government focus on internal reforms, and having secured entry
to the euro zone, time has provided the opportunity for the
vacuum to be filled.

The real opportunity to demonstrate that a new mood was
awake in Greek political circles came with the devastating Turkish

earthquake in August 1999. The immediate response of help and support from the Greek Government and the outpouring of sympathy and help from ordinary Greeks across the country made a considerable media, political and emotional impact throughout Turkey. The Turkish response to the earthquake that followed some months later in Greece demonstrated that such generous human support would elicit a previously unknown warmth of response. The so-called 'earthquake dialogue' (now termed the Papandreou–Cem dialogue) that then developed between Papandreou and Ismail Cem, the then Foreign Minister of Turkey, contained the seeds of change.

The dialogue did not produce immediate or dramatic changes, nor was it expected or intended to. If relations were to be altered after decades, even centuries of hatred and conflict, it would not happen quickly. The dialogue was, however, fundamentally important.

Firstly, if it was to have had any potential, it had to be ring-fenced from the ongoing cut-and-thrust of Greco–Turkish politics. In other words, no crisis in relations could be allowed to close down the dialogue. Those engaged in it needed trust and confidence in each other to keep it going.

Secondly, it offered the chance for dealing with some low-level issues before they developed into major issues and potential conflicts. Thirdly, it was an illustration to the wider international community that there were politicians in both Greece and Turkey who were prepared to take a chance, and not inconsiderable personal political risks, for the longer-term good of both countries and the wider region. Fourthly, it was a powerful demonstration that leadership can be exercised from within the region, and need not depend on power-brokers from outside. Lastly, the development of trust and confidence even on low-level issues was a strategic approach, designed to take time, seize opportunities where they arose and run with them. If it worked it would eventually represent the spirit in which some bigger issues would be tackled. That could only happen once the dialogue had matured and developed, but offered ultimate hope for discussion on issues like the territorial disputes in the Aegean and the Cyprus problem.

Amongst the Greek Cypriots, and sometimes even Turkish Cypriots, the frustration at the slow pace and exclusion of the Cyprus problem from this dialogue was almost palpable. That frustration had to be understood in the context of one community, the Greek Cypriot, that saw a developing relationship between its major supporter and its so-called enemy, and the other, the Turkish Cypriot, that had a strong sense of time slipping through its fingers, and feared the submerging of its own cultural identity and the loss of control over its own community affairs. However, Cypriot leaders, both Greek and Turkish, understood that the dialogue had to be in the best long-term interest of Cyprus and the wider region. As for the wider international community, it fully supported the dialogue and respected the need for care, caution and considerable patience.

The full consequences of the collapse of the Turkish Government during the summer of 2002 and the consequent resignation of Ismail Cem as Foreign Minister, have still to be analysed. Not enough time has yet elapsed to be sure whether the dialogue can be sustained in the context of the new majority Islamic Government of Turkey. The dialogue, with its potential for the future, needs another Turkish interlocutor, or it might have to be put on the back burner for the foreseeable future.

However, the Turkish Prime Minister Abdullah Gül is an intelligent and astute political player. He previously held ministerial office in the short-lived Erbakan Government led by the Islamic party Refah, which was subsequently removed by pressure from the military in 1997.

During one of my visits to Turkey during the Erbakan administration, I met with Gül. In fact, it was he who had arranged for me and my delegation to be received by a senior general of the Turkish Military High Command. Requests for such meetings were a regular part of our pre-visit schedule, but until that moment had always been rejected by previous governments. In discussions with Gül, he was clear that access to the military was important if Turkey's friends in Europe were to understand the nature of Turkish democracy and the role of the military in underpinning that democracy.

Incidentally, it was that same Gül, at that same meeting, who made the argument that his Refah party had more social-democratic policies than Turkey's traditional social democrats, and added with a grin that perhaps Refah should apply for membership of the Socialist International!

During the years since Greece entered the EU there was often a general, if unstated, feeling of exasperation in the international community about Greece, its political processes and its preoccupations. Whether warranted or not, and however fair or not, that sense of exasperation was often projected onto anticipated Greek responses to political questions of the day. The message of that unspoken ambience transmitted itself to Greek politicians and often, through insensitive press comment, to the Greek people. All of the events described above had combined to begin the process of changing that perception in the corridors of power in Brussels and in the national capitals of the Member States of the Union and beyond. There was no question but that the storing up of goodwill towards Greece amongst other European leaders would be important for the future.

Prime Minister Simitis was also constructive during the difficulties caused by the decision of the President and Government of the Republic of Cyprus in 1997 to order Russian-built S300 missiles for the defence of Cyprus. That decision nearly resulted in a major schism between Cyprus and its European partners and the US. Whilst the US had accepted the need to talk to the Europeans about Cyprus joining the EU and indeed then sought to seize the moment to pursue its strategic objective by driving the European governments to bring Turkey closer to the European family – it was not prepared even to discuss the issue of whether Cyprus needed the S300 missiles or not. The position of the US was absolutely firm – the missiles could not be delivered to Cyprus.

For the first time in seven or eight years, an action taken by the Government of Cyprus caused considerable consternation and opposition in the European Parliament. The political groups that had been united for years on a common policy to support Cyprus's right to join the EU were now equally united in their judgment that bringing a strategic missile system to Cyprus would exacerbate the arms race on Cyprus and destabilize the progress of the Republic of Cyprus towards membership of the EU.

The Union was, however, also dismissive of what appeared to many to be an inappropriate response from Turkey, which was threatening to blow the ship carrying the missiles to Cyprus out of the water! For Turkey, the crisis represented an opportunity for it to score a major diplomatic success in its relationship with the

EU. It failed to capitalize on it because it chose the propaganda route, rather than making its international representations and media statements in more measured tones, and using reason rather than threats. A little more foresight might have given Turkey a considerable political advantage; it was, after all, an issue that Turkey was always going to win.

The international community set to work to find a way out of the problem. In one initiative I met with the British Foreign Secretary Robin Cook on the sidelines of a meeting of the Socialist Group in Brussels, and asked him to use his best offices to provide an initiative through the UN Security Council, or through a Clinton–Blair transatlantic statement reiterating support for a solution to the Cyprus problem, and indicating that international efforts would be rededicated to that end. The hope was that such a statement would at the very least provide the opportunity for the Government of Cyprus to welcome and support the initiative, thereby creating the basis for the postponement of the delivery of the missiles.

Clinton and Blair subsequently made such a statement, which proved to be one part of the process that helped agreement to be reached between Simitis and Clerides for the S300 missiles to be, in effect, parked on the Greek island of Crete rather than going on to Cyprus. Greece had understood the diplomatic issues at stake and, given the strong external imperatives, had responded with pragmatic proposals for ending what could have been a real threat of war in the waters of the eastern Mediterranean.

Turkey's concerns about the military balance of power in the region had undoubtedly influenced the US and EU policy-makers. At the same time Greece was also beginning to demonstrate its capacity in the international community, responding to issues and international questions with a growing sense of maturity that was understood by the power-brokers. She was also bringing to the table a sense of creativity and flair that managed to combine the best elements of the passion of Mediterranean politics with a strong strand of pragmatic good sense. That Greece had found some in the Turkish political elite expressing a readiness to engage with this agenda was fortuitous and, more than anything else on offer, provided hope for the future.

The relationship between Greece and Cyprus had traditionally, of course, been close. The culture, religion, language and history shared by Greek Cypriots and Greece had played a pivotal role in the evolution of modern-day Cyprus.

The traumatic period in July 1974 of the coup against the then President of Cyprus, Archbishop Makarios, instigated by the dictatorship of the Greek colonels, caused a major and catastrophic division between the two countries. The failure of the coup, as Cypriots fought off the forces which had landed and attacked the President's official residence, led directly to the Turkish invasion of the north of Cyprus. The ceasefire in Cyprus in August 1974 left the country divided and devastated. The consequent collapse of the dictatorship of the colonels and the restoration of democracy in Greece gradually saw the re-establishment of peaceful and friendly relations between Athens and Nicosia.

Today, whilst the relationship is close, the previously vocal calls for Enosis (union with Greece) that underpinned the attempted coup in 1974 are only heard from a tiny minority of extremists, and are dismissed by the community at large.

Cyprus functions as an independent country. Its leadership and bureaucracy are overwhelmingly of indigenous Cypriots, as is its economic life. It has an independent currency and stock exchange. Its education system owes as much to the British colonial legacy as it does to Greece, as do many of the country's laws and civil procedures. Its armed forces train and are supported by specialist advisers from Greece, but they remain relatively few in number, especially when considering the scale of the militarization of the island.

Clearly, in terms of international political partners, a special relationship exists between the Governments of the Republic of Cyprus and Greece. In any progress towards the solution of the Cyprus problem Greece remains a critical player. The strengthening relationship of Greece with its partners in the EU cannot be other than useful to Cyprus in its efforts to become part of Europe. Similarly Greece's dialogue with Turkey can only be positive in the search for a solution to the problem of Cyprus.

8 The challenge for Turkey:

European values or historic enmities

Any argument which proposes that membership of the EU would be a positive force for the reuniting of Cyprus must pay heed to the fact that Turkey is a major player in that scenario, and needs to give particular attention to the relationship between the EU and Turkey.

Similarly, it is impossible to start exploring and understanding that relationship without first reverting to at least a cursory reminder of the age-old struggle for dominance in the eastern Mediterranean between Greece and Turkey. For the purpose of this study it is not valuable or necessary to delve into the history of that struggle, but it is necessary to evoke it, and to keep it very much to the fore as the issues are developed. There is no question that much of what has happened in relation to Turkey and Europe, and Cyprus and Europe, has its genesis in that historical enmity.

As with so many other conflicts over borders and resources in the eastern Mediterranean and the Middle East, the present-day protagonists are either trapped by, or resort to, the propaganda value of many of the historical arguments, events and incidents lying behind those conflicts. What is worse is that they all too often go on to superimpose those arguments on twenty-first century problems, making inevitable certain responses from 'the other side', based on a partial or tendentious representation. Underlying much of this is a religious xenophobia that is an irrevocable and unique part of the region's past and present.

The region itself would have enough internal strife, neighbour-to-neighbour, if left to itself. But when one adds the interplay of major international powers, the boiling-pot becomes a cauldron. For a variety of reasons ranging over the centuries, from apparent religious fervour to cynical manoeuvring over energy resources, the 'big' players have sought to dominate and/or divide the region in their own best interests. Promises made to indigenous peoples over centuries by the major players have been discarded as vested interests demanded. Colonial relationships have been overwhelmingly exploitative and often cruel. Regimes have been sustained by one foreign backer and undermined by another. The region's history is still a living history, and modern-day national and political leaders live with the historical mistrust, jealousies and intrigues.

Turkey and Greece are a major part of that cauldron which is the eastern Mediterranean, and suffer too from a deeply ingrained and skewed historical national understanding of their neighbours. In an environment of this sort, it takes an extraordinary individual to transcend that mindset, and exercise a different kind of intellectual and leadership pattern. That at the beginning of the twenty-first century some remarkable initiatives have emerged owes much to the courage of individuals in the political hierarchy of both Greece and Turkey. Those initiatives carry the potential for making such change.

Turkey has had a long-established relationship with the EU. Indeed it established its European vocation first in 1959 with an application to join the EEC, and then with an Association Agreement signed in 1963 and a further protocol in 1973 setting out its route to a full customs union. The early stages of that agreement were carried through, but the various military interventions in the democratic processes of the country slowed down progress, at some points to a standstill, and it largely drifted into the sands.

Furthermore, in 1987 Turkey applied for membership of the EU. Although at that time it was rejected for a variety of reasons, this was an important moment, as it defined Turkey's right to apply for membership, and by virtue of accepting the application as valid and asking the European Commission to report on the application, the Council of the EU clearly acknowledged that Turkey was a potential Member State of the Union and had the right to make such application.

In the light of the comments of some politicians and some national media during the 1990s, it is important to remember that Turkey's right to apply was established many years ago. It is also critically important to remember that the Treaty of Rome and its subsequent amending treaties certainly make no mention of a criteria of membership based on the predominant religion of the applicant state. Those who argued that a predominantly Muslim state should be disqualified from membership of the Union were not only wrong in terms of equality, democracy and fairness, but were wrong in law. There is also an overwhelming case to be made in contradiction of such a view, albeit a more subjective one, on the morality of such a position.

It is true that the EU has, however, never defined the scope of its boundaries. It has never attempted to gauge where Europe begins and ends. With the inclusion in 1995 of three of the four Nordic countries (the exception being Norway), with the candidacies of the Baltic states, the Balkan states, Turkey, Cyprus and Malta, the question of Russia and even the former eastern republics of the Soviet empire cannot currently be ruled out at some time in the future. Notwithstanding that discussion, Turkey was clearly accepted in 1990 as a potential member of the European family. The declaration at the European Summit at Helsinki in 1999 that Turkey was now to be included as a candidate country was once again reiterated, and confirmed Turkey's right to expect a European future.

It is the fact of Turkey's clear eligibility for membership of the EU that has defined the way in which the institutions of the EU, and particularly the European Parliament, have approached Turkey in the last decade.

As the case for Cyprus's membership of the EU grew and the island's application was given a positive Opinion from the Commission and Parliament, followed by the target date and then the opening of negotiations for membership, the rhetoric against Cyprus's being allowed to join the EU grew more, and yet more, strident in Turkey. Turkey acquiesced to the demand of the Turkish Cypriot leader Denktash that relations between the EU and the north of Cyprus should cease until the negotiations for membership with Cyprus were suspended. It supported the insistence of the Turkish Cypriot leadership that no further talks on a solution to the political problem should take place until the north of Cyprus was recognized as a separate independent state, and it argued that Cyprus should not join the EU unless Turkey itself joined at the same time.

The last point was an important one, and requires considerable and in-depth examination, because in some circumstances it was a seductive argument. It was also one that appeared to have been marketed strongly to the US administration by Turkish politicians, diplomats and, one suspects, the Turkish military.

The argument was seductive because it appears on the surface to be fair. It offers an apparently balanced and just approach to dealing with the issue. With Greece already a member of the Union, nothing could seem cosier and more designed to offer a solution on all fronts, that is to facilitate a solution to the Cyprus problem, ease tension between Greece and Turkey, and allow peace and stability to evolve in at least one part of the troubled wider region.

However, for the EU Cyprus was just one of the issues that presented a problem for Turkish membership of the EU, and it was arguably far from the most important. To claim that Turkey and Cyprus could join the EU at the same time was simply an argument manufactured to appeal to those who were dealing with just one facet of Turkey's problems, and quite deliberately to draw a veil over other fundamental difficulties with which the EU and Turkey were grappling. It was either an attempt to use the international drive to solve the Cyprus problem, by establishing an untimely and premature relationship between the EU and Turkey, or an attempt to delay the accession of Cyprus for the foreseeable future. It is important, therefore, to explore some of the outstanding issues of Turkish democracy and civil and military construction that remain a large part of the problem.

Turkish democracy, as established in its Constitution, allows for the armed forces of the state to sit outside of the democratic control of the nation's civil authorities. The military has exercised a dominant, and in some cases decisive, role through the National Security Council established by the Turkish Constitution. This is quite contrary to the situation of those democracies within the EU which insist on civil control of all military and security forces. It is, therefore, a critical issue for Turkey's European partners.

In Turkey the military is charged with the guardianship of the secular nature of the state. Hence Atatürk established the division of state and Islamic authorities that became such an important feature of Turkish democracy. In a region of the world where religion and state has been disastrously intertwined even in modern history, this has given Turkey a marketable reliability, particularly in European and US eyes, and allows it to claim to be the bulwark against perceptions, real or otherwise, of the westward creep of political Islam.

However, the military's political power has without doubt been the single most important factor at the heart of the frailty of Turkish democracy and the weakness of the political structure and system of government. On four occasions in the last 60 years the Turkish army has intervened against the directly elected Government of Turkey. The first occasion was on 27 May 1960, when the army moved against the Government of Adnan Menderes. The Prime Minister himself, Foreign Minister Fatin Zorlu and Finance Minister Hasan Politkan were hanged for violating the Constitution after the military took control. Both the second and third military interventions were against Governments of Süleyman Demirel, once on 12 March 1971 and then again on 12 September 1980. The fourth occasion was when the High Command moved in an informal, more subtle but decisive manner to force the Islamic-based Erbakan Government out of office in 1997, providing direct evidence not only of the continuing constitutional power of the army but also of the weakness of the political process and the immaturity of the structures of civil society.

The stability and robustness of Turkey's democracy is, therefore, a direct concern for the EU. Were it to be a member of the Union, Turkey's leaders would, quite rightly, be sitting at the same table as the leaders of some of the oldest and certainly the biggest democratic states in Europe. They would be sharing the decision-making about the future shape and direction of the Union. What is more, the size of Turkey's population would determine that under the European Constitution it would be wielding a large number of votes as one of the largest Member States. The possibility that Turkey's leaders could, under some circumstances and on some issues, be under the constraint or influence of its generals is a distinct possibility that the EU cannot ignore.

Any suggestion that the rights and responsibilities given to the Turkish military in the Constitution of 1923 may be window-dressing, or part of the preamble to the Constitution, is simply unsustainable. Firstly, the military is proud of its constitutional role, and takes it very seriously, and secondly, the evidence of the past 50 years is clear proof of the real intent and use of that role.

The headquarters of the Turkish High Command in Ankara on 24 March 1997 was the venue for perhaps one of the most unusual meetings I undertook during my time in the European Parliament. General Çevik Bir, a leading Turkish general recently returned from a stint as the officer commanding the UN force in Somalia, met a delegation I led from the Socialist Group in the European Parliament. We had specifically asked for permission to meet with the Turkish High Command to talk through some of these wider democratic issues as well as touching on both the Kurdish and the Cyprus problems. According to Bir, the National Security Council was made up of equal numbers from the Government and the High Command. He made the case that the National Security Council makes recommendations to the Government, and went on to say to an astonished European delegation: 'Do you know what? The Government has never once refused a recommendation of the National Security Council'!

A major issue, therefore, remains for European democracy in accepting into membership a state that could be constitutionally challenged by its military at any time. Conversely, it cannot be ignored that the Turkish constitutional provisions have probably prevented the state adopting a more extreme Islamic Government in the recent past, although many would argue that a debate is needed about whether the Turkish Islamic model can genuinely be compared with that of Iran or other fundamentalist movements. Whatever the conclusion of that particular debate, the European family must give serious consideration to the significant political value of these constitutional provisions that without doubt secured secular government in modern Turkey. The EU will have to balance this considerable added value against the democratic issues thrown up by a military that is not under the control of civil society, as is the norm in European democracies.

However, the weakness of the Turkish democratic process cannot be entirely explained away by the constitutional role of the military. In any state that has a democratic foundation, with a constitution that has been in place for some seven or eight decades, it would have been normal to see the development of a vibrant civil society. With a functioning party-political democracy (excluding the military interludes), Turkey could have been expected to generate the usual range of non-governmental and voluntary-sector pressure groups. As is normal in a democracy, such groups could have expected to develop a defined interaction with government and a respected role in society. Their leaders could have expected a certain status in the wider community and to be consulted extensively in the evolution of the domestic policy agenda, from businessmen and -women to trade unionists, through civil liberty and equality campaigners to those interested in minority and gender issues. Many of these community leaders would unquestionably have become active in the political process, and have taken leading roles across the economic, social, cultural and political scene. However, Turkish civil society is surprisingly underdeveloped. This became a further major issue in the debate on the nature of Turkish democracy within the institutions of the EU, and the European Parliament in particular.

Whilst Cyprus is certainly a political issue that stands in the way of Turkish membership of the EU, there is another: the Kurds. The European Parliament has been vociferous in support of the rights of minorities around the world. It could not, and neither should it have, ignored clear infringements of the civil and human rights of a minority in a country that was actively seeking to become a member of the Union. The political issue of the Kurds remained unresolved, and the Turkish authorities refuse to accept it as an issue to be discussed in membership negotiations with the EU. And yet the Member States of the Union have to deal with tens of thousands of Turkish Kurds entering their territory as illegal immigrants, requesting political asylum and living as refugees within the borders of the EU. It is clearly an issue that must be resolved, not only because of its implications for EU states, but for the internal politics of Turkey and the maturity of its domestic structures and its relationship with its own people.

The treatment by Turkey of its minorities in general is yet a further democratic issue for the EU in its membership negotiations. In this Turkey is not alone. The EU has pursued exactly the same issues with, for instance, the Baltic states and their Russian minorities and the Czech and Slovak Republics and their Roma communities, as well as working with the Hungarian and Romanian Governments about the Hungarian minority community in Romania.

Turkey is different in one respect, however. It refuses to accept that the EU has a legitimate interest in these issues. Whilst the other candidate, or even initially pre-candidate, states mentioned above work with the Union to bring their minorities legislation into line with that of the Union, ensuring all the time that it respects their domestic history and present conditions, Turkey was and remains antagonistic to any suggestion that it needs to address the minority issue. In an EU whose ethos is developing with quite remarkable speed into that of an organization of Member States with a growing regional geography often determined by a minority ethnicity, the candidacy of a strong centralized government that actively denies the existence of minorities in its territory presents a further obstacle to membership.

Whilst consistently and frequently condemning terrorist campaigns, the European Parliament was keen to support the ordinary Kurdish families who had been and were still being displaced in huge numbers by the Turkish military's policy of burning the villages of the Kurdish people to prevent them becoming safe areas for those fighting the guerrilla or terrorist war. As the Parliament tried to direct its funding resources to NGOs working with the Kurdish people rather than through the Turkish state, the difficulties between the Parliament and the Turkish Government grew.

The European Parliament saw both the need for funding to help the development of civic society and the difficulties surrounding funding for the Kurdish lands as particular weaknesses. It determined to use the European funding resources available to it, or over which it had influence, to support the development of civil society in Turkey through support for NGOs. The Turkish authorities took extreme dislike to the advocacy of the European Parliament on behalf of Turkish groups outside governmental control. They resisted the distribution of funds to non-governmental groups, and sought allies in the European Commission to try and circumvent the democratic controls being exercised by the European Parliament. Rumours circulated in the Parliament that the Commission, in response to Turkish overtures, was encouraging the emergence of 'paper' NGOs seemingly fully detached from the control of the Turkish state, but which were in reality vehicles through which to launder EU funding for government-sponsored projects. Whilst none of these rumours were ever authoritatively proved, they were persistent and added to the sense of distrust and antagonism between the Parliament and the Commission.

The Commission, aware of its multi-layered agenda with Turkey and under pressure from its Member States and from the US, which was stepping up the pressure on both the Commission and individual governments, found itself between the devil and the deep blue sea. An angry Parliament accused the Commission of working hand-in-glove with the Turkish Government to establish new client NGOs through which European funding could be laundered to the projects of the Turkish state, both in the Kurdish lands and more generally. Delegations from the various political groups of the European Parliament were visiting Turkey to meet with the NGOs and visit the Kurdish areas almost monthly. Anecdotal evidence and rumours were accruing of European funding being allocated to human-rights groups in Turkey but never finding its way to the bank accounts of those groups. The mood between the European Parliament and the Commission became increasingly sour, especially after the attempted assassination of one of the most prominent leaders of a Turkish human-rights group.

As is usual with the EU, some of the most innovative developments occur at times of crisis between the institutions. In a remarkable move, the Parliament exercised its leadership and constitutional powers by seeking a meeting between the President of the European Commission, Jacques Santer, the Commissioner responsible for foreign policy in this area, Hans Van den Broek, and the leaders of all seven political groups in the Parliament. After some tough negotiations, Santer agreed to the establishment of a joint Commission–Parliament working group of two senior people from each institution. That working group examined and approved or rejected every single future funding application for Turkey, and also dealt with the huge back-log of applications that had become frozen during the dispute.

Such powers had never been exercised by the Parliament previously, and marked its growing strength in its relations with the

Commission, and the development of its role as the body to which the Commission was accountable. Parliament would not have its role as the only democratic institution of the Union thwarted by the bureaucracy. It also demonstrated that the Parliament considered the development of the relationship with Turkey to be critically important if Turkey was to be a member of the EU. This was an important moment for both the Commission and any state wishing to enter the Union. The nature of European parliamentary democracy had begun to exert itself.

All this demonstrates that the Cyprus problem is far from the only issue that stands between Turkey and early membership of the EU. Perhaps as important as the substantive issues is the question of understanding, acknowledging and respecting the norms and values of the club that one seeks to join. The EU is the most sophisticated and developed regional political body ever developed. It is a body made up of independent states coming together from strength, and having expressly agreed to pool some of their sovereignty for the greater good of all. It is axiomatic, therefore, that a state expressing an intention to join such a club and putting great energy into arguing for its candidate status should be prepared to adopt that same philosophy. For such a state then to expend great energy in an attempt to halt the membership of another sovereign state, whose application to join has been acknowledged to be valid, must surely create a sense of unease and generate some considerable misgivings.

So, for Turkey the vigorous and vocal campaign to prevent Cyprus joining the EU must be counter-productive in efforts at garnering friends across the Union. To invoke the power of the US, generating a sense that one has powerful friends 'over the sea' that support a particular application regardless of rhetoric at home, is a dangerous game to play in the European context. The European political scene is not simple. Before a new country can join the Union, it requires firstly the satisfactory negotiation of entry terms, which will take years even in the best of conditions, secondly the approval of the European Parliament, and finally that of national parliaments as well.

The European Parliament is a complex organization. Whilst the parliamentarians come from the Member States whose governments, at least whilst sitting with the governments of other

Member States in the European Council, have presumably approved the membership application, they are not all, of course, sympathetic to their own governments, coming as they do from across the political spectrum in their own domestic political environment. The British Labour MEPs in fact formed the majority of British representatives during the last 10 years of the Conservative Government in Britain, and used every opportunity to undermine decisions made by that Government, with which they fundamentally disagreed. Given that Labour MEPs sat in the largest political grouping in the Parliament, and were the single largest national delegation within that grouping, they were able to have some considerable successes.

So the battle to gain the majority support of the European Parliament should not be taken for granted. It is also not unknown for some Member States to prefer to see a decision made in Council defeated by the Parliament, even if it had had their silent support in the Council. With parliamentarians sitting in multi-national political groupings, such machinations are perfectly possible, and part of the cut and thrust of politics in Europe.

If the hurdle of approval by the European Parliament is cleared, the membership of any applicant country has to be approved by each national parliament in each Member State before the process can be completed. Even if rejection is unlikely, a national parliament is capable of inflicting a humiliating delay in the process. Once again, national parliaments need to be part of the consideration of any applicant state.

There was, therefore, a considerable leap in understanding necessary in Turkey if, during the years of discussion and negotiations for membership, a general sense of confidence and partnership was to be established with the institutions of the Union, the existing Member States, their parliaments and amongst the European citizenry generally. By the end of 2001, that campaign had not yet begun.

If any doubt existed about just what a mountain Turkey had to climb in that respect, the details in the following chapter of the struggle for the introduction of the customs union between Turkey and the EU are demonstration enough.

9 An ever closer union:

what price a customs union with Turkey?

In the second half of 1994, the Turkish Government reactivated its request to update and complete the customs union with the EU. This had been signed in 1973 but had drifted off course during Turkey's periods of military dictatorship. It became clear very quickly that this was perceived in Turkey as a truly important part of the country's short-term objective to set its face to the west rather than the east, to root its democracy within the wider European context, and in so doing to enhance its standing and respectability in the eyes of the powerful Western international community. Turkish politicians across the political spectrum overwhelmingly supported the request. The diplomatic corps drove the request hard in the institutions of the Union and in each national capital of the Member States of the Union. The military threw its weight behind the drive for membership. In the European Parliament, the lobbying strategy of the Turkish Government was professional and effective. Using top-notch international lobby firms in the Saatchi and Saatchi mould, Turkey was promoted through glossy leaflets and regular updating bulletins. The country's diplomats conducted regular rounds of senior parliamentarians and pursued their case with vigour. It was a united attempt, and a hard sell.

However, by 1994 the original customs union was significantly out of date and inappropriate. Calls for its completion demanded a total overhaul of the original agreement. That in turn activated the full decision-making process through the institutions of the EU.

On the surface, having completed the process once before, that should not have presented too much of a problem. However, in the intervening years much had happened in Europe. Firstly, the Union had expanded to 12 Member States, and was destined to be 15 on 1 January 1995. Secondly, amongst those who had joined the Union in those years was Greece. Thirdly, the European Parliament that had agreed the original customs union with Turkey had been unelected, with its members appointed from national parliaments. Since 1979, the Parliament had been directly elected, with the members having a personal and direct mandate from the electorate. The Parliament's role and rights had also grown considerably. It could no longer with any justification be called simply a rubber-stamping exercise.

The myriad pressures grew on the European Council and Commission. How to keep the Turkish Government happy? How to take the Greek Government along with the flow in the Council, and avoid it exercising its veto? How to manage the issue of Cyprus, whose application for membership was also before the Council for reassessment, and was actively opposed by Turkey? How to satisfy a European Parliament that was strident on the rights of the Kurds, and adamant on the rights of Cyprus to join the Union? At the same time, the Turkish Government had been a staunch ally in the Gulf War, the US was keen that Turkey should be more closely allied with the European family, and Turkey itself felt it deserved to be treated well, given its role in the Gulf War and its geostrategic importance in the region.

On 16 February 1995, in the run-up to the important General Affairs Council meeting on 6 March 1995, the European Parliament formally advised the Council that the time was not right for the completion of the customs union, 'as the human rights situation in Turkey was too serious' (Resolution B4-1530/rev.). The Parliament appealed to the Turkish Government and Turkey's Grand National Assembly to undertake a fundamental reform of the Turkish Constitution in order better to guarantee the protection of democracy and human rights in Turkey, and to contribute to a solution of the Cyprus problem.

It was a sensitive and complex situation, and much hinged on just how the Greek Government would act in the Council meeting. With the Parliament clearly having stated in advance its opposition to the customs union with Turkey, it would have been easy for the Greek Government to have played an obstructionist hand, had it wished.

The Council meeting ended with the historic agreement that formally endorsed Cyprus's application to join the EU, and gave the start date for the opening of negotiations with Cyprus as 'six months after the ending of the inter-governmental conference'. This was important for two reasons. On the one hand, it gave the clear go-ahead for Cyprus to become a member of the Union. Once negotiations had begun, it would be extremely difficult for the Union to stop the process. If the Government of Cyprus carried out all the negotiations for entry, and proceeded to bring its own domestic laws into line with the Union's acquis communautaire, which was in itself no small task and would entail a considerable financial cost, then, save a major schism of some sort between Cyprus and the Union, it would be inconceivable that the Union could withdraw its support for Cyprus's membership.

On the other hand, the fundamentally important part of the agreement of the meeting on 6 March 1995 was the Council's commitment to complete the customs union with Turkey. The importance of that commitment was that a customs union was perceived to be the closest possible relationship with the Union other than full membership. It demonstrated that Turkey was also set on the road to membership of the Union, even if the timescale was still to be determined. It basically put into place a more profound relationship between the Union and Turkey across the spectrum of economic and fiscal activity and opened up the other areas of policy for discussion.

If not formally linked in the Council statement, however, what was evident was that this double commitment for the eastern Mediterranean had clearly been the result of a political deal reached between the government leaders meeting at the Council. It was also clear that Greece had not only lifted its veto on policy related to Turkey, but that the Greek delegation had played a significant part in constructing and negotiating the deal. This was confirmed in private discussions that I had with Yannos Kranidiotis, the head of the PASOK delegation in the European Parliament, who had accompanied the Greek Foreign Minister Theodore Pangalos to the Council meeting on 6 March 1995.

Whilst repeating that the Council did not formally link the two agreements, the French President in Office of the Council, Alain Lamassoure, was quite explicit when he made his report to the European Parliament on his return from the Council. Responding to a question from a parliamentarian, Lamassoure, on behalf of the French Presidency that had chaired the Council meeting on 6 March, made clear the nature of the political deal and the consequent commitment of the European Council and Commission to both Turkey and Cyprus.

All parties (with the exception of Turkey and the Turkish Cypriot leadership) expressed themselves satisfied with the decision. In effect, the Council had confirmed that Cyprus was now in an identical position to the leading candidates from Central and Eastern Europe and the Baltic states.

Negotiations could not begin with any of them until the conclusion of the inter-governmental conference called to deal with the difficult institutional and political issues that had to be addressed before yet more countries could enter the Union. Outstanding issues related to voting strengths in each of the institutions, the streamlining of the decision-making process to accommodate a Union of 20–25, the number of commissioners that would make up the future Commissions, the balance of powers between the large, the smaller and the micro states, and so on. The discussion on those thorny problems all had to be underway before the Union could possibly have opened negotiations with any applicant state. After the Member State governments had agreed the new Treaty, it too was subject to ratification by the European Parliament, and then the potentially lengthy procedure of ratification by every national parliament. But regardless of that constraint, the Union was determined to open negotiations with the first tranche of applicant states six months after the formal ending of the conference. Cyprus's place in that queue was already certain.

So with the issue of Cyprus's membership of the EU now secure, and safely parked until six months after the ending of the inter-governmental conference, the institutions turned their attention to the completion of the customs union with Turkey. This was to develop into a protracted attempt to exercise leverage on Turkey, and a major and defining issue of confidence between the institutions of the Union.

The Council's decision had placed the ball firmly in the Parliament's court, as it was now required to ratify the customs union agreement by vote in a plenary session. That was not to be as easy as it might have appeared on the surface. No single political group in the Parliament had an absolute majority. The political groups created majorities by seeking out allies in different groups, or portions of groups, who could be relied on to vote a certain way depending on the issue. Finding a majority for the customs union with Turkey was going to be very difficult, given its delicate nature, the different issues involved and the diversity of views across the Parliament, to say nothing of some covert discrimination amongst some parliamentarians, albeit a minority. There were also complex national sensitivities as well, touching on levels of migration and growing fears of xenophobia.

The predominant concerns of the Parliament with regard to Turkey were concentrated on three main fronts: firstly, internal democracy in all its manifestations; secondly, the treatment of the Kurdish people and the Turkish attitude to minority and human rights in general; thirdly, the Parliament could not accept that a country which maintained a large force in occupation of an independent country, and come to that a country that was also an applicant state of the EU, could join the Union until that problem was solved.

The virtual unanimity of the large number of British Labour members in the European Parliament on the Cyprus issue came into play at that point and largely determined the strategic approach for the Socialist Group. What was important to me in that discussion was that nothing was done that would put in jeopardy the opportunity for Cyprus to open negotiations with the EU. If Boutros Boutros-Ghali was right, and the only cards on the table as far as Cyprus was concerned were European, then that hand of cards was to be played through.

The Government of the Republic of Cyprus was extremely circumspect during the months in which the debate raged in Europe and Turkey on whether or not the Parliament should ratify the customs union with Turkey. Whilst delighted that Cyprus had been given the open door to membership of the EU by the decision of 6 March, it was very keen not to be seen engaging or involving itself in the debate on the customs union. This, it was argued, concerned the relationship between the EU and Turkey, and on this the Republic of Cyprus would not comment.

The decision of 6 March was controversial amongst Greek and Turkish Cypriot citizens and residents within the EU. Some in the Greek Cypriot community could not understand any approach that was designed to give anything to Turkey. They saw anyone who could vote in favour of the customs union as betraying the cause of Cyprus, and some were vocal in their condemnation. That section of the community was not able to see, or accept, the longer-term strategic aim of forcing open the window of opportunity for a solution to the Cyprus problem that the drive for Cyprus's membership of the EU would offer.

Conversely, Turkish Cypriots, even those who were overwhelmingly in favour of EU membership for Cyprus, were understandably anxious about a deal which allowed the Government of the Republic of Cyprus to open negotiations for EU membership without the views of Turkish Cypriots being heard. They feared that it might be used as an excuse to drive the north of Cyprus further into the hands of Turkey and undermine the Turkish Cypriot identity even more.

As the discussions in the European Parliament went on, and real dialogue with the Turkish authorities opened up, it was, however, the reaction of a certain section of the mainland Turkish community in Britain that became the focus for interest. Upset that the European institutions should question and criticize the role and actions of the Turkish Government, that section of the Turkish community began a vicious and malicious campaign against me and some other European MPs and the European Parliament in general. That campaign continued for some 18 months and involved threatening letters, abusive newspaper articles, crude caricatures, demonstrations and even the delivery of a black wreath to my office in London.

The Turkish Kurdish community that lived within the EU, particularly in Germany and Britain, were also very vocal on the issue of on just what terms Turkey ought to be granted the customs union. By the end of the process, the two major concentrations of Kurdish opinion, which spanned both countries, were split on their approach, with one group arguing strongly to oppose ratification because not enough had been achieved to put right some of the worst excesses of the Turkish state. The other argued equally strongly that enough progress had been made, and that the European Parliament should ratify the customs union. By so doing, it argued, the EU would maximize its future influence with Turkey, whereas rejection would simply end it.

However, whilst the concerns of the various Cypriot and Turkish communities in Europe were very time-consuming and complex, they were as nothing compared to the battle royal that was going on in the European institutions.

Whilst the desired strategic result was clear to see, the tactics of securing it were going to be difficult. If the majority of the European Parliament was to vote in favour of the customs union, it could not be done unless Turkey was to make some important concessions. The four leaders of political groups of the left-wing parties in the Parliament that commanded a majority of the votes met to consider their position. I had instigated a private monthly dinner meeting with the three other leaders of the left when I was elected head of the Socialist Group in 1994. By the time of the customs union issue, we four leaders had come to know and understand each other. We had developed a considerable rapport that stood us in good stead during this and other periods of stress in the five years from 1994 to 1999.

Alonso Puerta, the Spanish Leader of the Communists, Claudia Roth, the German Leader of the Greens, and Catherine Lalumière, the French Leader of the Radical Group, and I kept in close and careful touch during the next nine difficult months. On some occasions we talked with Gijs de Vries, the Dutch Leader of the Liberal Group, who on issues of this nature often held similar views. We shared a common agenda: to stimulate and support real change in the domestic situation in Turkey that would demonstrate that a new agenda was developing in Turkey, led by Turkish politicians, in short to show that Turkey was capable of sustainable internally instigated reforms of its Constitution, its penal code and its approach to political dissent, political prisoners and torture in prisons.

The tactics were based on the view that if domestic changes of that sort could be driven by Turkish politicians with the backing and support of the institutions of the EU, then progress towards not just the customs union but eventual membership of the Union

for Turkey could be unexpectedly rapid. Even more exciting was
that if such changes could genuinely be carried through, they
would create a tremendous amount of goodwill towards Turkey in
the international community, and help to create an environment
in which both the Cyprus and the Kurdish problems could begin
to be addressed on a more rational and mature basis.

Over the following nine months the issue of Turkey and its
relations with the EU dominated the foreign-policy work of the
Union. The Foreign Policy Committee of the Parliament discussed
every angle of the proposed customs union in depth. Such was the
intensity and sometimes acrimony that the Joint Parliamentary
Committee (JPC) made up of representatives of the European
Parliament and the Turkish Grand National Assembly had to be
formally blocked by the Parliament. Time-consuming efforts had
been made in order for agreement to be reached on an agenda for
the meeting of the JPC that would facilitate discussion on the sensitive issues on which the Parliament needed clarity. The members
from the Grand National Assembly simply refused to have them on
the agenda, let alone talk about them. The Parliament would not
sanction a meeting at which its concerns could not be raised, and
the JPC was blocked for months and months. However, political
group meetings in the Parliament received the leaders of their sister
parties in Turkey and had frank and open discussions with them.
Political leaders from the Parliament visited Turkey for formal
discussions with the Government, senior members of the Grand
National Assembly, prominent civil servants and diplomats.

On one, now infamous, visit to Ankara, Claudia Roth, Catherine
Lalumière and I represented three of the four left-wing groupings
and carried with us the political support of the fourth. That was
an important visit, as it demonstrated the unity of the left that
carried the majority vote in the Parliament. The Turkish media
followed the three European political leaders around Ankara ob-
sessively. Amongst others, we had a long and difficult meeting
with Tansu Çiller, the Turkish Prime Minister, which focused
particularly on the campaign against the Kurdish terrorists and the
impact on Turkish attitudes to minority and human rights.

Although starting badly, with the Turkish Prime Minister deli-
vering a monologue on the evils of terrorism, once we had opened
up the debate it did at least end with a better understanding of the

issues confronting both Ankara and the EU. I made the arguments to the Prime Minister that whilst we understood her need to manage her political and public constituency with care, particularly given Turkey's fragile relationship with the military, we also needed to manage our political and public constituency with equal care. We argued that Turkish political leaders needed to recognize that fact as legitimate. It would then be easier for the Turkish authorities to engage in compromise during discussions and negotiations, rather than insist on a simple 'winner takes all' position.

After that visit to Turkey, there was a considerable amount of press coverage. One article in particular engendered international condemnation when it quoted a Minister of State in the Çiller Government, Ayvaz Gokdemir, with whom we had not even met during our stay in Turkey, as saying that Turkey should not pay any heed to 'the three whores from Europe'! The resulting outcry in political circles in the European parties and in the Turkish press resulted in apologies from both Tansu Çiller and the hapless minister. Whilst both Catherine Lalumière and I declined to take the issue further, Claudia Roth instituted a legal case against the minister, which she eventually won in the Turkish courts.

Although the level of contact and discussion with the Turkish authorities was immense, that with the European Commission was even greater. The Commissioner himself was obliged to report regularly to the full plenary session of the Parliament that met monthly in Strasbourg, as well as to the Foreign Policy Committee of the Parliament. He also had regular private meetings with the political leaders in Brussels and Strasbourg in an effort to keep everyone up to date and aware of progress.

For the Parliament's political leaders, who represented major European political families, discussion was also held at the very highest level with the leaders of their national political parties. I recall a caucus meeting of socialist/social-democrat prime ministers during the Spanish Presidency of the EU in 1995. With Spanish Prime Minister Felipe Gonzáles in the chair, the discussion turned to the customs union. The prime ministers present were clearly in favour of their parliamentary group ratifying the customs union, whilst I made it clear to them that opinion amongst their national delegations in the European parliamentary group was split, and was at that stage clearly favouring rejection.

After six or seven months of intense activity, the Parliament's position crystallized around demands for a handful of reforms from the Turkish authorities as a demonstration that they were serious, and determined to continue down the reform road. However, the Parliament was confronted with a procedural problem of how to force a debate onto its formal agenda to allow the full plenary session to give real authority to its calls to the Turkish Government. On 15 November 1995, the Parliament tabled a motion to unblock the JPC. That had three objectives: it broke through the procedural log-jam and allowed the Parliament to have the issue of relations with Turkey on the agenda at a strategically important moment; it provided an opportunity for the Parliament to indicate unequivocally just what action it perceived as vital if the vote on the customs union, scheduled for just four weeks later, was to be successful and to give the Turkish authorities focus as they sought to complete their reforms; and it allowed the JPC to meet and the deputies from both the European and Turkish Parliaments to have a long overdue discussion on the issues.

That debate left the Turkish Government in no doubt about just what was required from it. Each of the requests for action was based on aspirations that had been raised by the Turkish authorities themselves. They had proclaimed that they were seeking to change their penal code. They had insisted that such changes would be accompanied by releases from prison of many political prisoners. They had promised to extend the electorate to include Turkish nationals abroad. They had wanted to remove the ban from political office that currently existed for civil servants and trade unionists.

In essence, none of the requests laid out in the Parliament's debate were simply dreamt up by idealistic or unrealistic parliamentarians. In a host of formal and informal talks, the Turkish authorities had laid out their package of reforms and promised that those changes would be forthcoming. The Parliament wanted them to be in place before the vote on the customs union as a demonstration of will and progress rather than just talk of future action.

With the Parliament's position clearly outlined some four weeks before the final vote on the customs union, tension eased briefly. The final days were, however, frenetic as the Turkish authorities began to respond to the Parliament's resolution by placing the reform package before the Grand National Assembly. The European

Commission chased the political group leaders for their responses and thoughts on progress – was it enough?

For her part, Çiller conducted a whirlwind charm offensive at European prime ministers. Arguing strongly that Turkey was at the forefront of the struggle against Islamic fundamentalism, she urged them to put their weight behind an appeal to their national MEPs to vote in favour of the customs union. I received two approaches from the UK Government seeking my active influence on the Socialist Group for a positive result to the ratification process. The first was a phone call from Tony Blair, then Leader of the Opposition, on whom Çiller had called during her visit to London to see Prime Minister John Major. The second was an invitation to meet with Foreign Secretary Malcolm Rifkind for a discussion on the current situation on Turkey. As one of the key players in the Parliament on this issue, and one of the instigators of the strategy, I was able to outline to both of them my approach and the direction in which I was sure the Parliament was headed.

As the vote drew near, the Grand National Assembly had before it the reform package, which included the critical elements for the European Parliament. At the same time the release of prisoners began in Turkey, first a trickle and then, by Turkish standards, a veritable flood. By the time of the vote, 142 political prisoners had been released from Turkish prisons. Ankara had clearly pulled out all the stops to set the right mood music for the vote.

On one particular day in the weeks preceding the vote in Strasbourg, I was engaged in a hectic day of meetings and speeches in my North London constituency. As I drove from meeting to meeting, the Turkish Prime Minister was chasing me on the telephone. When we did manage to speak on the fringes of a meeting, she told me that she had done everything she could to persuade her MPs to vote for the critical reform package. 'I have been down to the Grand National Assembly and taken tea with the deputies,' she claimed, adding, 'I don't think I can do anything else now'!

In the two or three days before the vote in the European Parliament, the political leaders on the left met to decide whether enough had been secured to recommend a vote in favour. I was prepared to recommend that the Socialist Group vote in favour, and Puerta and Lalumière agreed. Claudia Roth had to accept that her group was very evenly split, and she could not gauge how its vote would go.

In a heated and extremely difficult debate, the Socialist Group finally voted by a majority to support the customs union. Part of the deal to secure the positive vote was the agreement to establish 'Turkey Watch', a group of six senior group members, chaired by myself, to conduct detailed work on the internal developments in Turkey and report back to the whole group. Turkey Watch became a focus of interest for human-rights and associated groups throughout Europe, and played a major role in determining the political approach to all issues related to Turkey during the following three years.

On 13 December 1995 the vote to give assent to the customs union with Turkey was carried in the plenary of the Parliament in Strasbourg, with 344 votes in favour, including my own, 149 against, and 36 abstentions.

For the European Commission, this whole episode was a painful but useful experience because it established some parameters for the discussions with the other enlargement countries of Eastern and Central Europe. The Parliament's approach to the customs union was used, for instance, in discussions with the Slovak Government of Prime Minister Vladimir Meciar when it sought to make changes to the Slovak Constitution that would have limited the rights of minorities and moved the country towards a one-party state. These constitutional changes created a significant schism between Meciar and the President of Slovakia, who refused to put his signature to them. As Slovakia was a candidate country of the EU, the European Commission and the Parliament were, by reference to the Turkish example, able to demonstrate that those issues would become a significant block on Slovakia's route to the European family. Similar arguments were also made with regard to the rights and treatment of the Russian minorities in the Baltic states.

For the European Parliament, the whole period had marked a significant development in its relationship with the Commission and the Council. It could not have been made clearer that the Parliament would no longer be counted on just to vote as directed. That was, of course, the same Parliament that went on to make history by sacking that same European Commission in March 1999.

For Turkey, the political elite had also seen that the European institutions were something to reckon with. To their credit, they did start the process of reform, but sadly at that time never completed it. Some in Ankara may have thought that they had achieved their objective by securing the customs union, but in then reneging on the reform package by failing to bring to fruition elements of the penal code changes, not establishing the rights of trade unionists and civil servants to take part in elections, and even re-imprisoning some of the released, they did further damage to their longer-term political credibility and trustworthiness. In a later meeting that I had with Çiller in Ankara, when she was Foreign Secretary in a Government led by the Islamic party, Refah, she had the grace to accept that Turkey had not carried out all the promised reforms.

It is noteworthy that since EU agreement that it could become a candidate country for full membership of the EU, Turkey has claimed once again that it has another reform package and would this time carry it through.

10 Decision-making so far:

from Dublin 1990 to Nice 2000 via Luxembourg and Helsinki

The Republic of Cyprus moved forward so markedly in adopting the acquis communautaire that it was always likely to be among the first of the candidate countries to reach the finishing post, and be ready to enter the EU. Malta, the other Mediterranean island candidate, was also making reasonable progress in the negotiating process. If all else were normal, it would be a fairly simple task for both Cyprus and Malta to be admitted to membership of the EU easily and quickly. Both countries are ready; they have relatively sophisticated administrations still much in tune with Western European practices, given their long recent histories as British colonies. The amount of EU funding needed to support both countries would be tiny, and their admission would not affect voting strengths in the institutions in any significant way. They would be the easiest of all the current candidate states to admit on a purely technical and administrative basis. The question was whether the EU would be prepared to admit Cyprus without a solution to its problem.

To make a realistic, rather than an emotional, assessment of the answer to that question, it was necessary to look at the facts and the actual decisions made over time by those who would be required to make the final decision.

The European Council, in instructing the European Commission to open negotiations for Cyprus to become a member of the EU, set in train a tried and tested course of action. In Copenhagen on

12 December 2002 that course of action came to an end with the decision to admit the Republic of Cyprus to membership of the EU on 1 May 2004. The EU has never in its history opened negotiations with a sovereign state, taken it through the years of complex negotiation on the detail of the adoption of the acquis communautaire, concluded those negotiations successfully and then refused to allow that state to enter. It is true that Norway did not enter the EU after completing its negotiations, but that was due to the rejection by the Norwegian people of the terms of entry, not to a failure of the EU to admit the country.

All history and precedent dictates that the EU would have put itself at significant risk of a legal, if not constitutional, challenge if it had refused entry to Cyprus at the successful end of this process. Even more, it would constitute a damning indictment of its values and principles if it even contemplated such a move. It would also have given a very unwelcome message and shaken the confidence of other small and vulnerable candidate states about their place in the club if a country that had done everything that had been asked of it, and done it well, had been refused entry in such a way. This is not an insignificant concern to those states whose complex relations with Russia still remains a major factor for the future.

It is important to understand that the European Council has returned to the question of Cyprus regularly in its deliberations over decades, and particularly in the light of the next round of enlargement. On each occasion it has reiterated its support for Cyprus's membership of the Union in an unqualified manner.

The European Council, which meets usually four times but certainly twice each year in June and December at the end of each of the six-monthly rotating presidencies of the EU, has never exhibited a sliver of doubt that it was fully behind the efforts of the UN in its effort to secure a solution to the Cyprus problem. Nor has it taken even vaguely contradictory or confused decisions on its readiness to bring Cyprus into membership of the Union.

Even before the Government of Cyprus submitted its application for membership on 4 July 1990, the European Council had regularly discussed the Cyprus question in the light of the failure to make headway on a solution through the inter-communal dialogue. If any proof were needed that the prime ministers of the EU considered Cyprus a European problem, it is to be found in their regular and persistent statements expressed over many meetings.

Anyone seeking to establish the actual commitment of the EU at its highest level in support of Cyprus's application to join the Union could not fail to be struck by the consistency of approach and commitment made at virtually every meeting of the Council since the Government of the Republic of Cyprus submitted its application.

Similarly the Council has always understood that the problem of Cyprus has been and remains a significant factor affecting its desire to bring Turkey closer to Europe, and now of course to see Turkey become a member of the European family.

Three high-level meetings in particular are worthy of note because they more than all the others can be considered critical in endorsing the future vocation of Cyprus. They are the meeting of the General Affairs Council on 6 March 1995, the European Council meeting in Helsinki on 11 December 1999 and naturally the European Council meeting in Copenhagen on 12 December 2002.

The General Affairs Council meeting on 6 March 1995 reconsidered the application of Cyprus for membership of the EU. The Council, made up of the foreign ministers of the Member States re-examined Cyprus's application in line with its earlier decisions and the conclusions of the Corfu and Essen European Councils, and of course had before it the important report from the experienced EU observer for Cyprus, Serge Abou. That meeting reaffirmed the earlier decision about the suitability of Cyprus for accession to the EU and confirmed that the Council expected Cyprus to be in the next stage of EU enlargement. The Council of course expressed its regret at the lack of progress in the inter-communal talks which had just concluded without success in New York, and once again urged all those concerned to keep working at it. This meeting was also important because it articulated the case for the support that the EU would have available for the economy of the north of the island, and was explicit that this would be for the Turkish Cypriot community. The Council was clear that the Turkish Cypriot community needed to understand the full advantages available to it upon EU accession more clearly, and went on to urge the other institutions of the EU to improve and increase their links with the Turkish Cypriot community.

Perhaps the most significant part of this lengthy Council state-ment on Cyprus was the decision that accession negotiations should start on the basis of Commission proposals six months after the conclusion of the 1996 inter-governmental conference. This was the moment that all applicant states await. It is the point at which the road to accession is clearly set.

Helsinki on 11 December 1999 saw the European Council welcome the launch of the talks on 3 December in New York aimed at a comprehensive settlement of the Cyprus problem, and expressed its strong support for the UN Secretary General's efforts to bring the process to a successful conclusion. It underlined that a political settlement would facilitate the accession of Cyprus to the EU. In an important statement, the Council went on to say that if no settlement were reached by the completion of the accession negotiations, the Council's decision on accession would be made 'without the above being a precondition'. Once again this was a crucial statement in ensuring that the leverage provided by the application of Cyprus for membership of the EU remained in play and at the disposal of the Secretary General of the UN.

The final crucial meeting of the Council, which set the seal on Cyprus's vocation, was held in Copenhagen on 12 December 2002, and marked the closing of Denmark's six-month period in the chair of the EU. At this summit the 15 prime ministers had before them the recommendation of the European Commission for the next phase of the enlargement of the EU from 15 to 25 countries on 1 January 2004. The 10 next Member States are to be Poland, Hungary, the Czech Republic, the Slovak Republic, Slovenia, Estonia, Latvia, Lithuania, Malta and Cyprus.

For the remaining three, Bulgaria, Romania and Turkey, their future vocation as part of the wider European family has been reconfirmed. Both Bulgaria and Romania have the prospect of entry in 2007. As for Turkey, its continuing promises of internal reform were welcomed, and additional help and support promised by the EU. A date to open negotiations with Turkey is still to be decided. Progress will be reviewed in December 2004.

For Cyprus the record of commitment from the European Council, the highest-level decision-making body in the EU, is impressive. The body is, of course, made up of the prime ministers of the Member States of the EU. It was patently nothing other than a propaganda exercise to claim, as did some opponents of Cyprus's entry to the EU, that the Council is a tool of the Greek Government. It has, at meeting after meeting, made its position clear, and in fact in Helsinki in December 1999 was explicit about its position on the admission of Cyprus. The Helsinki statement confirming that a solution to the problem was not a precondition has been supported on many occasions since, both publicly and formally by the various government leaders, and now has been put into effect by the decision in Copenhagen.

It clearly remains the preferred option of the Council that Cyprus should enter the Union as a united country. In this context the detailed proposals put forward by Kofi Annan on Monday 11 November 2002 for a solution to the Cyprus problem are crucial.

The proposals deal with every aspect of the problem and lay out in great detail arrangements for the structure of a bi-zonal, bi-communal federation in keeping with the resolutions of the UN over the previous three decades. Issues of security, territorial readjustment, the return of refugees from both sides to their homes (or compensation), parliamentary structures and leadership of the country are all set out in complex detail.

The presentation of the 150-page document is the final piece in the jigsaw of the parallel model for the solution of the Cyprus problem. Without doubt, it marks the concluding chapter of the current international drive to bring together a solution with the entry of Cyprus to the EU. Accompanying the proposals was a tight timetable for the leaders of the two communities to put their signature to agreement that the text provides the framework for the future. The four weeks leading up to the Copenhagen summit on 12 December 2002 were designated for detailed discussions designed to allow the Council members to have confidence that a final agreement on the solution is within striking distance. In the event, negotiations did not take place within the timescale.

However, the Council statement records:

as the accession negotiations have been completed with Cyprus, Cyprus will be admitted as a new Member State to the European Union. Nevertheless the European Council confirms its strong preference for accession to the European Union by a united Cyprus. In this context it welcomes the commitment of the Greek Cypriots and the Turkish Cypriots to continue to negotiate with the objective of concluding a comprehensive settlement of the Cyprus problem by 28 February 2003 on the basis of the UNSG's proposals. The European Council believes that those proposals offer a unique opportunity to reach a settlement in the coming weeks and urges the leaders of the Greek Cypriot and Turkish Cypriot communities to seize this opportunity.

If there is agreement by 28 February, the Kofi Annan plan envisages a referendum in both communities in the first half of 2003 designed to secure agreement on both the solution and entry to the EU. If that all comes together as hoped, it will mark the success of a remarkable international initiative and demonstrate the value and influence of the new politics of the EU. Whilst the diplomatic drive to secure this end has really gathered pace in the last three to four years, the whole campaign began a full decade earlier.

During that same decade, the European Parliament became a powerful tool in the attempt to keep the issue of the continuing division of the island of Cyprus high on the international agenda. The early 1990s saw the Parliament seeking out appropriate opportunities to present to the Council and Commission the genuine issues which impacted on one or other of the Cypriot communities, through the lack of a resolution of the problem. Taking care not to adopt a scattergun approach of the sort that had alienated and sometimes irritated the wider international community over the previous quarter of a century, MEPs sought external drivers that created the right environment for action.

The sale on the international market of prized mosaics removed from Orthodox churches in the north of Cyprus provided the opportunity for debates on the destruction of the cultural and religious heritage of Cyprus. The work of the International Red Cross in seeking information and evidence on the fate of the missing people from both communities since the war in 1974 allowed debates and resolutions on the tragedy of the missing and the continuing anguish of their families. The work of the Council of Europe on the plight of the enclaved Greek Cypriots in the Karpas peninsula was the stimulus for an ongoing discussion on the nature of the prevailing democracy and respect for human rights in the north of Cyprus. The murder of a Turkish Cypriot journalist working on a newspaper that opposed the leadership in the north of Cyprus offered the chance for a statement on the repression of

Turkish Cypriot civil society. The bombing of the car and offices of a Turkish Cypriot opposition leader presented a chance to try to create an international network of support for such leaders by raising awareness of the intimidation to which they were regularly subjected. The series of major forest fires that destroyed large parts of Cyprus both north and south of the Green Line gave scope for major debates on the need for, and value of, united work on environmental protection and the potential for the EU to take a lead through its financial protocol with Cyprus. Decisions of the European Court of Human Rights on the rights of the displaced to their homes, businesses and produce were yet another chance to bring out a specific and little understood dimension of the division of the island.

Those were just a few of the targeted actions taken in the European Parliament that were the inspiration for motions, emergency resolutions, questions to the Council or Commission, or requests for statements from the President of the Parliament. Their focus and resonance with other international activities and the decisions of other international bodies ensured that they carried credibility and gravitas. The range of issues raised for both communities by the continuing division of the island gave ample scope for the regular highlighting of the problem through different but important routes.

In the latter years of the 1990s, the Parliament had legitimate internal cause for raising the island's problems through the emergence of the application of Cyprus to join the EU. But still the issues of missing people, refugees, human rights, political plurality in the northern part of the island, demographic changes, enclaved people and trade bans were real and continuing issues that would have to form part of any solution.

Throughout the 1990s, the Parliament made clear that Cyprus's vocation was in the EU and that it would support that position. In its report in 2001 on the application of Cyprus to join the Union the Parliament's rapporteur, the former Foreign Minister of Luxembourg and a veteran social democrat, Jacques Poos MEP, was unequivocal. He stated the Parliament's wholehearted support for the UN process and deplored the unilateral withdrawal by Denktash from the UN-sponsored proximity talks, urging him to engage in a new round. The Parliament put its full weight behind the

Helsinki formula whereby resolution of the Cyprus question was not a prerequisite for accession, and specifically ruled out the possibility of separate negotiations with the two parts of the island, or the accession of two Cypriot states, or the accession of the northern part of the island upon Turkish accession.

The Parliament's report was unambiguous in saying that if Turkey were to carry out its threat of annexing the north of Cyprus in response to EU membership it would put an end to its own ambitions of EU membership. Instead, it invited Turkey to regard membership of Cyprus as an important contribution not only to the secure existence and development of both communities but also to the welfare of all its citizens. It argued that the membership of Cyprus in combination with the demilitarization of the island and security guarantees by the EU would be an enormous step towards peace and stability in the region, and would strengthen the accession partnership between Turkey and the EU.

The characteristically robust report of the Parliament was adopted, with over 90 per cent of those Euro MPs entitled to vote casting a vote in favour. Poos was subjected to vilification in the Turkish press. He unhappily had cause to complain to the Turkish Foreign Minister about accusations that he had 'relations of private interest' with the Republic of Cyprus. Sadly, Turkish tactics remained the same, but with a different target. There was, however, little doubt about the commitment of the European Parliament.

In order to complete the ratification process for each new country to join the EU, the national parliament of each Member State has to endorse the treaty with each candidate country. Each Member State has its own process for the ratification of international treaties. These processes range from a simple majority vote in the parliament itself to the holding of a national referendum with a consequent parliamentary vote. This is a slow and cumbersome process, and can sometimes be subject to considerable delay and even rejection.

The ratification of the Maastricht Treaty, which whilst not of itself an enlargement treaty did deal with some of the changes of infrastructure needed to facilitate enlargement, was thrown into disarray when it was rejected by the people of Denmark in a national referendum in June 1992. In a tortuous procedure over the following months, the Danish Government negotiated a complex series of amendments that were acceptable to its own people and which could be tolerated by the other Member States of the EU. Once agreement had been secured with the EU, that agreement was itself put to another national referendum in Denmark before the Maastricht Treaty could come into being across the EU.

Similarly, the Treaty of Nice agreed by government leaders in December 2000, paving the way for the institutional change needed for future enlargement, was rejected in a national referendum by the Irish people in 2001. Whilst national ratification proceeded in the other Member States of the EU, Ireland engaged in a process of negotiation with its own people and other Member States to establish just what was necessary and possible if it was to have any prospect of securing positive support for the new Treaty from the Irish electorate. As in Denmark following the rejection of the Maastricht Treaty, a second referendum was put to the Irish people to secure their agreement for the Nice Treaty. The referendum held on 19 October was supported by the Irish people with a 62.8 per cent vote in favour, thus paving the way for the Treaty of Nice to come into being, allowing the constitutional changes necessary for the next phase of enlargement.

There have now been two clear cases which prove that it is impossible to pre-empt or accurately predict the responses of 15 national ratification processes, especially in those Member States that are constitutionally required to put any new treaty to a referendum of all their people. However, the national parliaments have always endorsed previous enlargement treaties of the Union without significant problems. It is true that some time ago the Dutch Parliament expressed its concern about endorsing the entry of a divided Cyprus. Given the collapse of the Dutch Government on 16 October 2001, just three months after its election, and the consequent dysfunction of the Dutch party political system, considerable delay in the ratification process in the Netherlands is not beyond the realms of possibility. However, it remains to be seen whether Dutch or any other national parliamentarians would actively vote against.

To make a judgment on whether the EU had the will to say yes to Cyprus is now academic, but it is noteworthy that at every stage of the process at which the issue was genuinely put to the test the EU, throughout its institutions, has said yes.

11 Future perspectives:

stability in the eastern Mediterranean

The enlargement of the EU is the biggest challenge confronting the governments of the EU. It represents a powerful component in the evolution of a peaceful and stable European continent in the aftermath of the collapse of the Soviet Union, and offers the potential for a prosperous and successful European economy in the global marketplace.

The EU began the latest enlargement in a hopeful vein, at the same time as the Euro was successfully launched and in the context of a strengthening European economy. It began in the firm belief that it would provide a process by which the new countries that have emerged from behind the 'iron curtain' would be firmly rooted in the shared democracy of the new Europe.

Along with that positive environment, there was inevitably a strong streak of political cynicism and manoeuvring as each European Member State sought to secure a firm advantage over its European partners by creating good relations with the larger candidate states, or at least those candidate states with whom they thought they could do business. Both Jacques Chirac and Helmut Kohl, for instance, laid great stress on an early entry date for Poland during their respective visits to that country to sell the value of EU membership, whilst of course maximizing the value of trade with their country, Jacques Chirac famously claiming that he thought Poland would be in the EU by 2002!

Such completely unrealistic optimism led to heightened expectations in the candidate countries and particularly raised public
opinion in a way that left it vulnerable to disappointment. When
the inevitable delays occurred this almost certainly contributed to
a down-turn in support for membership of the Union in some of
the candidate countries. At the time the European Parliament was
criticized in some of those same candidate countries for apparently
dragging its feet over enlargement and being less enthusiastic than
the other institutions of the EU. In fact the Parliament's assessment of the breadth and scope of the task in hand, the length of
time that would be necessary, and the difficulties that would be
encountered proved to be much more accurate and realistic.

As ever, when the economic environment is favourable it is
easier to take people and nations along with a visionary agenda
and an outward-looking scenario. So it was at the beginning of
the current round of enlargement.

Up to 2001, the negotiations progressed with the candidate
states, but at the same time the international economic situation
deteriorated. The continuing difficulties of the global economy in
the opening years of the third millennium and its hesitant and
sporadic attempts to lift itself out of the doldrums have exacerbated
the difficulties of persuading the public in current Member States
that it will be in their long-term interest to support enlargement.

The early rejection of the Treaty of Nice by the Irish people in
a referendum demonstrated the point. The Treaty signed by the
15 governments in December 2000 laid out some of the proposed
changes that were necessary to the existing EU Treaty in order to
facilitate this enlargement round. Ireland is one country that made
excellent use of the special funding regimes designed by the EU to
aid countries with a standard of living substantially below the EU
norm. The special funding was designed to help Greece, Spain,
Portugal and Ireland to raise their domestic standard of living
to the EU average. With the enlargement to Eastern and Central
Europe in particular, all four of those current Member States that
have been eligible under the present criteria for special funding
have to face the unpalatable fact that not only will they lose EU
funding support, but that some of them may also be required
to become net contributors to the EU budget in order to extend
special funding support to the new Member States. The economies

and standard of living of the Eastern and Central European candidate countries are at a significantly lower level than any of the
current Member States. With an economic down-turn affecting
the European economy, it is not surprising that the arguments for
enlargement are proving difficult to sell at home.

This pinpoints one of the major conundrums that both current
Member States and increasingly the candidate countries must solve.
The EU is eminently political. Enlargement is not just a simple
technical evolution. It is about the development of the EU space.
It is about bringing European countries together in a shared space
that respects identity, diversity of culture, language and tradition,
in order that the promises of long-term peace, stability and economic growth can be secured. This in turn requires the support of
the citizens of the Member States of the Union. The overriding
danger for the evolution of the EU and perhaps to its very existence
is the dangerous slide in popular support amongst its peoples. The
European project carried popular support at its inception because
it offered something different after a calamitous Second World
War. In essence it was a visionary political concept that carried the
business world with it because of its commercial good sense and
the strength of its business offer.

The energizing success of that business offer in the mid-1980s
became so powerful that it carried the concept forward to unex-
pected heights – the Single Market and then the single currency.
The reality of both the Single Market and currency followed closely
on the heels of the worldwide information-technology boom that
has revolutionized every aspect of business and has driven the
creation of the global marketplace. The EU has developed an
agenda designed to give European states a better-than-average
chance of succeeding in a dynamically changing world. However,
its internal public relations have not kept pace with its rapidly
evolving political and economic profile. It is only latterly that EU
leaders have woken up to the need to secure the popular backing
of citizens for the project. But even now, instead of making the
case in each country about the crucial need for Europe to succeed
as a common venture if it is to have a unique selling point in the
global market, the leaders of each state have continued to use
Europe as part of their domestic political power struggle. This has
been the consistent failure of the political process in the Western

European democracies. The shock of the Danish rejection of the Maastricht Treaty ratification process and more recently the Irish failure to ratify the Nice Treaty, taken together with the diminishing electoral interest in the European Parliament throughout Europe, has finally generated a sense that, at the very least, European public opinion has to be more carefully handled. The leap of faith to actually selling the European project in an exciting and appropriate manner for today's world still remains for the future.

If the extended business offer is to be successfully achieved and its resultant prosperity harnessed, however, Europe's leaders increasingly need to secure the agreement and goodwill of their citizens for the benefits of a wider Europe. The EU is not like any other international organization. It cannot be understood in the context of NATO, a mini UN or NAFTA. It is about changing national attitudes and behaviour to other nations, or it is nothing. Changing attitudes through political action has become part of the stock in trade of the EU over the last decade. Those who believe that Europe is just a trade organization have simply lost the European plot.

Take the example of the EU's Mediterranean policy. It is designed to bring the leaders and governments of the countries bordering the southern coast of the Mediterranean into constructive discussion and synergy with the EU. The practical reasons for developing such a policy are that the problems of the countries of the southern coast of the Mediterranean are European problems. Failing economies brought about by war, civil conflicts, lack of democracy, mismanagement, corruption, poverty and deprivation have already forced the mass exodus of refugees from those countries into the EU. The problems associated with mass migration are a growing trauma in and between EU Member States. Similarly the drugs and vice trade that have developed routes from those countries into the EU have provided a second imperative for action of some sort. The EU's response has been to develop a three-part Mediterranean policy. The first and largest part is the economic support package, designed over time to help put the economies in question back in some sort of order. But tied to that economic package is a democratic package focusing on helping to develop and extend democratic participation in each country. The third part of the package is a security dialogue bringing the countries together with the EU in an attempt to explore the wider security issues of the region, and to reduce and ultimately eliminate smuggling in drugs and people. So the sweetener for change is the large economic package, the lever to access that package is democratic evolution and action on security and illicit trades.

Yet a further example of the manner in which the EU's profile has become more overtly political, and geared towards changing behaviour and attitudes, particularly in the states in its own back yard, was the initiative in the mid-to-late 1990s by Greece to encourage the EU to develop a Balkan policy. Its aim was to mirror the Mediterranean policy in order to provide some similar incentives in what was becoming an increasingly tense part of the world, and also from the clear standpoint that the problems of the Balkans would inevitably become European problems. Since the conflicts in the former Yugoslavia, the EU has moved with speed and money to develop that Balkans policy and is, with the UN, a key provider of support, both financial and human, to develop civic society and democracy as well as the regeneration of the economy, whilst NATO keeps the peace.

In this context, the EU is developing an approach to its unwritten sphere of influence that mirrors more ruthlessly that of the nation state. The extent of Europe's involvement and level of commitment of resources and funding in any of the continent's problems is based primarily on an assessment of its vested interest.

The same analysis holds true for both Cyprus and Turkey. Europe has a powerful vested interest in both as future members of the club, and is therefore prepared to put significant resources into both. In its dealings with both countries the EU has endeavoured to create space for innovation in the relationship.

In the formal constitutional context, Europe has insisted that in terms of membership of the Union, its relationship and negotiations with the Republic of Cyprus has nothing to do with Turkey. Similarly, it insists that its relationship and negotiations with the Government of Turkey have nothing whatsoever to do with the Republic of Cyprus. Given that the EU is governed by a written Treaty, there can be no argument with the contractual strength of that position. However, as argued earlier, the European Council, the apex of the EU, is eminently political. The Council recognizes that a political problem has existed between Turkey and Cyprus for decades, and has consequently tried to use the processes of negotiation for membership of the Union to create a unique symbiosis between the two states. Given goodwill and a legitimate desire and genuine commitment to solve the problem this approach could pay dividends for both countries. But it does require both to come to the table with a common understanding that this process could work and is worth working hard for. Both countries would find an EU ready to work with the US and the UN to secure the result that would guarantee long-term peace and stability in Cyprus and in the region.

At all times in this process the European institutions have tried to reach out to the Turkish Cypriot community and its leaders. Continuing efforts have been made to bring knowledge and information about the EU and the state of negotiations for membership to the north of Cyprus, despite the refusal of the leadership to take part in the process. With the exception of the period during which EU representatives were declared *persona non grata* in the north of Cyprus, there has been a steady stream of officials at all levels visiting the north. There have been seminars for businesses, meetings with political leaders, conferences for trade unions, press conferences and numerous meetings with local groups as well as with the leadership of the Turkish Cypriots. The will of the EU to involve the Turkish Cypriots cannot be in question, despite the acknowledged difficulties created by what the international community sees as the illegitimate nature of the regime.

The European Council and Commission prevailed on the Government of the Republic of Cyprus to secure an invitation for the Turkish Cypriots to take part in the process of negotiating Cyprus's membership of the EU. Nothing could make more sense than for both communities to have been represented in the negotiations. Given real goodwill and a commitment to walk the oft-repeated talk in favour of a settlement, such an active experience of working together could have proved a catalyst for the parallel course for a solution to the national problem of Cyprus. The invitation was issued by President Clerides on the eve of the European Conference in London on 31 March 1998, but rejected by Denktash.

On every occasion when members of the European Parliament asked for support for a community event to develop the relationship with Turkish Cypriots or for common Greek Cypriot and

Turkish Cypriot events, the European Commission has willingly agreed and supported with funding, speakers or other help. On one level, therefore, it is difficult to understand the constant stream of refusals and rejections from the current Turkish Cypriot leadership as anything other than an attempt to stall progress and generate an unnecessary and unprovoked crisis.

There is, however, a rationale to the Turkish Cypriot position. For Denktash the tactics of delay and obfuscation have a purpose. He has argued that the recognition of his 'separate state' is an essential precondition to a solution and that a solution must precede entry to the EU. His positioning is designed to keep up the maximum pressure for recognition of his state. Such a recognition would be a win–win situation for him. He would either strengthen his hand in any subsequent negotiations with the Greek Cypriots, or if that failed would have achieved the status he has so long craved. For Turkey, the moves towards a solution of the Cyprus problem did not assume critical level until it became the cause of constant pressure from its friends in the US. There is increasing evidence that this pressure grew strongly in the closing years of the 1990s and the opening years of the 2000s. Turkey's economic problems, combined with its real desire to become a Member State of the EU, have similarly generated significant and increased pressure from Ankara on the Turkish Cypriot leadership to become more open to the overtures from the UN.

Since the early 1990s the leaders of Turkey have declared themselves in support of the UN process to solve the problem of Cyprus. And yet until the closing years of the 1990s they took a less than enthusiastic view of attempts by the UN, or the EU working in close partnership with the UN, to make progress on the solution.

There are those who argue that the genesis of this approach is not based in Ankara, but with the Turkish Cypriot leadership. All the evidence indicates the opposite. The almost total financial and economic dependence of the north of Cyprus on Turkey alone clearly indicates that it would be difficult for it to exist if Turkey took it upon itself to withdraw. It clearly will not do so, but there can be no doubt about where the power resides. In confirmation of that fact, on 10 September 2001 the then Turkish Prime Minister, Bulent Ecevit, said publicly that Denktash consults with Turkey before making decisions about whether or not to accept the invitations of the UN Secretary General to attend inter-communal talks.

On this occasion Denktash refused to accept Kofi Annan's invitation to go to New York on 12 September, despite having made very positive statements about his pre-meetings with both Kofi Annan and Günter Verheugen, the EU Commissioner for Enlargement. Turkey strongly supported that action and clearly encouraged Rauf Denktash in his refusal.

Such was the frustration about this behaviour that two indige-nous Turkish Cypriot political parties, led at the time by Mehmet Ali Talat and Mustafa Akinci, criticized Denktash for not accepting the invitation, and even Turkish mainland newspapers were moved to write:

> What kind of Cyprus policy do you call this? Everybody knows we have a saying, 'play to lose'. That exactly sums up our Cyprus policy. An incredibly flawed policy. A policy that gives us one hell of a headache. Denktash's not joining Annan was a spectacular own goal for Turkey [Sedat Sertoglu writing in *Sabah*, Ankara edition, 9 September 2001].

Murat Karayalçin, a former Turkish Foreign Minister, is reported as telling the Turkish newspaper *Yeni Safak* on 11 September 2001 that he did not consider Denktash's withdrawal from the talks a positive step.

Yet the EU continues to pursue the complex negotiations with both countries in the firm hope that Turkey and Cyprus will acknowledge that there is a real opportunity for progress, and that the domestic vested interests of both countries would eventually prevail.

Now that the EU has said yes to Cyprus, the concern must be whether there is any aggressive intent from Turkey, given its oft-stated threat of 'serious consequences' if Cyprus is admitted to the EU. Turkish leaders have made this proclamation publicly and repeatedly, from the Prime Minister and Foreign Minister downwards.

There are several issues that have to be addressed here. Firstly, how can it be explained that a candidate country believes it has the right to issue such statements designed to prevent the admission of another candidate country? Secondly, why does Turkey perceive Cyprus's entry to be such a threat to it? Thirdly, what are the 'serious consequences' they speak of, and should the EU have cause to worry?

It is questionable as to whether a country whose political leadership expends much time and effort to try and prevent the EU admitting another sovereign country is itself ready to join the EU. The concept of conducting business in the EU by using this type of behaviour is anathema to many engaged in the European institutions. It is completely contrary to the concept of European integration and the philosophy of the EU's founding fathers. Whilst some may view this as irrelevant in the 'real' world, it is a truth that those engaged in the European institutions are often motivated and driven by this wider view of the future of Europe and the opportunity it offers for stability and peace. It is, therefore, to Turkey's considerable disadvantage that its politicians do not appear to understand the nature of the disservice they are doing to the perception of their country in the EU by such actions.

The hidden feature underlying this reaction, however, is a reflection of the lack of confidence of Turkish politicians in their ability to engage constructively in the debate on the solution of the Cyprus problem. It may be that this, in itself, is a reflection of the weakness of Turkish democracy and its political process. Nonetheless, it demonstrates a worrying lack of responsiveness that does not bode well for dealing with the sensitive and complex negotiations that frequently require the ability to compromise in the European Council and throughout the institutions of the EU. The politics of the EU are specifically not conducted in a 'winner takes all' environment.

Perhaps just as worrying is that the political elite in Turkey may feel an imperative to engage in these tactics to assuage the views of their military overseers. Cyprus is an important post to the Turkish military. During a visit to the British army in the buffer zone in Cyprus that runs between the Turkish and Greek Cypriot lines, I was shown a hillock extensively armed by the Turkish army. This place was described by the officer conducting the tour as 'one of the most fortified hillocks in the world and frequently used as a showcase by the Turkish military to dignitaries from foreign armed forces'.

As well as being genuinely reluctant to reduce or withdraw its forces for reasons of strategic strength and potential pressure in any future sensitive periods in the relationship with Greece, the Turkish army also values the opportunities that Cyprus offers in its military relationship with the US.

Conversely, nothing would give greater strength to the notion that Turkey is ready to join the EU than a clear shift of position to a genuine dialogue with the UN and the EU on a solution for Cyprus. The opportunity for Turkey to exercise some leadership and vision on the Cyprus problem exists, and would have a disproportionately positive effect on the image of Turkey in the international community.

In other words, the Cyprus problem can be viewed as a positive lever for Turkish relations with the EU. Cyprus, as a united country, could present a Turkish bridgehead into the EU. If intelligently argued, the conditions applicable to the Turkish Cypriot community could offer some important precedents for language, religion, culture and process which would facilitate the discussions with Turkey itself. Until now the Cyprus application to join the EU has, almost without fail, been perceived in Turkish quarters as a blunt instrument to be used for driving a wedge between Greece and the EU, or to try to force Turkish entry simultaneously with that of Cyprus. Turkey fears that Cyprus, as currently constituted, would represent a second government in the EU which would undoubtedly vote against Turkish entry. If the Turks are using Cyprus as a lever for their own entry into the EU, it is not surprising that they play that card – which some might view as their strongest negotiating asset – for all it is worth. But if a negotiating hand is not played intelligently and subtly, its value to the player is much diminished.

The second question relates to whether Cyprus's membership of the Union genuinely creates a difficulty for Turkey.

In this context it is important to remember that the overwhelming number of Turkish Cypriots favour Cyprus's membership of the EU. It is, of course, certainly true that its incumbent leadership has never accepted the application of the Republic of Cyprus on behalf of the whole island. The legal arguments about whether or not the Government of the Republic of Cyprus had the constitutional power to apply on behalf of the whole island are made extensively in other publications. The EU and its Member States, understandably, accepted entirely the existing position on the legal status of the island articulated by the UN. This is the position recognized by every country in the world with the exception of Turkey, that there is only one legal government in Cyprus, that of the Republic of Cyprus. Whilst Denktash and his supporters do not accept this reality, it remains the internationally agreed position, and has been so since 1974. The EU also recognizes that for the time being the Republic of Cyprus does not have control of the territory north of the Green Line. The UN has provided a formula for ensuring that the Turkish Cypriots continue to have a voice as a community, effectively and pragmatically ignoring the establishment in 1983 of an illegal state in the north of the island.

So what is the concern of Turkey about Cyprus joining the EU?

For Turkey as a state, the long-term effects of a united Cyprus in the European family should be positive. The burden of support that it currently carries for the economy and people of the north of Cyprus would be hugely, if not fully, reduced. The political burden that has attached to Turkey in its dealings with other governments and in international fora would not only disappear, but would be replaced with an acknowledgement of its role in supporting a solution. A significant burden of regional stress that the country currently carries in its relationship with Greece would disappear. Finally, one hurdle in their negotiations for membership of the EU would be lifted.

There are some short-term negative factors. Turkey would have to handle the sensitive job of persuading the present Turkish Cypriot leadership that it is in its best interests to be constructive, and be prepared to keep that leverage in place throughout the process. It would have to use its persuasive powers on its military High Command to persuade it that it is in Turkey's wider and long-term interest to secure a solution. If necessary it might have to call in some of the external influences on the military, such as the US. Perhaps the unspoken worry comes back to an earlier comment about an inherent lack of confidence amongst the Turkish political elite. Turkish politicians may have a sense that their leverage over the EU in terms of Turkey's membership of the EU currently resides in attempts to be difficult over the membership of Cyprus. They may fear that with Cyprus united and within the EU, those forces in the EU antagonistic to Turkish membership, for whatever reason, may reappear in a more significant manner.

This is a genuine point, and if truly reflective of a significant strand of political thought in the EU is a view that will have to be sorted out before Turkey joins the EU, regardless of the membership of Cyprus. This is also an argument in which Turkey would find itself with allies in the institutions of the EU which at this moment it believes to be its political enemies. Large swathes of the European Parliament, and at least some of the governments of the Member States, would not and could not allow themselves to be painted into the corner of religious intolerance and active discrimination against a Muslim state. The domestic implications in several of the Member States could be to exacerbate considerably tensions and inflame minority ethnic and community relations. And if there were truly to be significant numbers of those in the institutions or the Member States of the EU who would fundamentally oppose Turkish membership of the EU on the grounds of religion or culture, it must surely be true that those same forces would certainly not concede Turkish membership in order to allow membership for tiny Cyprus. So this is an issue that is going to have to be faced if it proves a serious reality.

What are the potential problems generated for Turkey when the Republic of Cyprus joins the EU if a solution to the Cyprus problem has still not been secured?

The resulting problems in this scenario are almost all self-generated for Turkey. Initially there will be domestic political damage. All recent Turkish governments have put much stock in preventing Cyprus entering the EU before a solution, or without a common membership date for Turkey and Cyprus. The Turkish leadership would, therefore, be subject to the internal criticism of its own press and media, with the consequential impact on public opinion. The subsequent problems would begin with the understanding that Turkey would have a continuing support role for the north of Cyprus for the long term. The prospects for a solution will certainly not be enhanced in the immediate aftermath of Cyprus's accession. Turkey's current financial, economic, diplomatic and political problems would be exacerbated by this prospect.

The final question concerns the regular warnings from Turkey of the 'serious consequences' that would result from the EU admitting Cyprus to the EU before a solution.

Turkish spokesmen have been careful not to be specific about the nature of the consequences. They have spoken initially about the full integration of the north of Cyprus into Turkey, in essence its transition to a province of Turkey. The reality is that the north of Cyprus is already very much integrated with Turkey. It is totally dependent on Turkey for funding short-falls. It uses Turkish currency and its population holds Turkish passports. It trades out of Turkish ports and cities, and its local services are overwhelmingly dependent on Turkish funding. There is already free movement of people between the north of Cyprus and Turkey, and the 115,000 mainland Turkish settlers are supported and housed in the north of Cyprus and have the right to vote there. There is very largely a customs-free relationship between the two. It may be that there are still some areas of activity that are not totally integrated, and in terms of the political relationship there is a facade of independence that would be lost. The real losers in any attempt to close any remaining gaps in the integration of the north of Cyprus and Turkey would be the indigenous Turkish Cypriots themselves, whose legitimate claims to a specific cultural identity, traditions and history would be further eroded. These are the very people whose interests Turkey purports to be defending.

A second scenario that has been floated, not by Turkey but by some in close touch with it, is that Turkey may try to blockade the island of Cyprus. The recklessness of such an act in such a sensitive part of the world not only seems destined to start a regional conflict but seems wholly out of proportion in cause and effect. If such a course of action ever seriously looked possible, then those choosing to continue to arm and give support to such a regime would have to look closely at their responsibility for world peace.

One certain response to any action by Turkey to annex the north of Cyprus or take any other course of retaliatory action against Cyprus would be to end, for the foreseeable future, its own chances of becoming a member of the EU. That would be a tragedy in terms of the potential for the stability, peace and development of the region.

The advocates of the parallel course for a solution of the Cyprus problem and entry to the EU have always anticipated and expected that as the conclusion of negotiations with the Republic of Cyprus drew near and the decision was made there could be increased and heightened tension and/or a drive towards a solution. In the final analysis it is clear that in the coming year, as we move towards the actual entry date of 1 May 2004, there will be both. With progress towards a solution very slow, and with time running out, there has been a series of inopportune statements, veiled threats and even some sabre-rattling from Turkey. However, there has also been an increased drive by the international community to establish talks between the two communities. In this all the indications are that Turkey appears to be playing a more helpful role by ensuring that the Turkish Cypriot leadership understands where Turkey believes its own political interests lie. In so doing Turkey may at last begin to help establish an atmosphere conducive to progress. It is still to be seen whether the Turkish Government elected on 3 November 2002 will develop and build on this trend.

It is a fact that if the political will can be generated on both sides a solution to the Cyprus problem could be secured quickly. The problems are not new. The proposals are already articulated and mostly uncontroversial. It is not beyond the wit of the experienced leaders involved to secure a solution within weeks.

A successful conclusion to the problem of Cyprus would engender the first hopeful sign of new life in the region. The scope for the development and success of the eastern Mediterranean would be considerable, and the leadership potential it would offer for the wider region immense. A solution to the Cyprus problem would be only a first step to a lasting peace, but it would be a powerful step. Finding a solution is not the same as a lasting peace. Whilst considerable effort has been made by international bodies – ranging from international trade unions to peace institutes, women's organizations, professional bodies and the like – to bring the people of Cyprus together, such efforts could only ever affect the minority. Learning to live together will be slow and tortuous, and there will be many obstacles. Trying to find the right language of conciliation and compromise in the education process, and seeking to counter the corrosive effect of more than three decades of propaganda will be a challenge that will require support and understanding from both communities inside Cyprus and from the international agencies and friendly neighbours in the EU and beyond.

However, a united Cyprus in the EU, and Turkey with a clear path to membership, offers the tantalizing prospect of Greece, Turkey and Cyprus co-operating together inside the EU. Therein resides the real hope for stability in the region. It would be a key contributor in helping Greece and Turkey to put aside their regional competitiveness and begin to develop synergy for the development of the region in and through partnership in the EU. Such a symbiotic relationship would be helped and supported by the other EU Member States. Then the EU really would be able to offer something more substantial to the wider region through its members with significant expertise and knowledge of the region, its strengths, weaknesses and political structures. Even the like-lihood of such a possibility should be enough to ensure that the players in the game should not allow the problem of Cyprus to stand in their way.

For Cyprus, its EU vocation is now certain. Since detailed negotiations were opened in March 1998, its record as a candidate country of the EU has been without parallel amongst the 12 other candidates. Its civil service and government bureaucracy has performed well in introducing the complexities of the acquis communautaire to the Cypriot statute book. Its politicians have worked in harmony with the EU Member States in international fora, and it has invited the Turkish Cypriots to engage with them in the EU negotiations. Its people remain steadily in support of the country's European destiny. It has done all that has been asked of it at virtually no cost to the EU. It has an economy that performs above the European average, providing a good standard of living for its citizens, and it is well placed to join the single currency. The decision at Copenhagen is confirmation enough that all of this is accepted by the EU.

On the parallel course being pursued to find a solution to the Cyprus problem, the Cypriot Government has attended every meeting to which it has been invited be that in Cyprus, New York or anywhere else. It has met with the growing host of special rep-resentatives for Cyprus named by individual governments, the UN, Council of Europe and EU. It maintains its support for the position so far agreed between the two Cypriot communities in support of a solution based on the UN resolutions in favour of a bi-zonal, bi-communal federation.

In the time between the decision being made to admit Cyprus to the EU and its actual entry, the EU will have to redouble its work with its partners in the UN, US and Turkey to secure agreement on a solution to the Cyprus problem: a solution that will allow the Greek Cypriot and Turkish Cypriot people to begin the process of living together in one country; a solution that will remove Cyprus as an issue in Turkey's relations with the rest of the world and allow it to continue down the road to its own membership of the EU; a solution that will provide greater stability and peace in the eastern Mediterranean, and allow the potential for better relations between Turkey and Greece to flourish; a solution that will demonstrate to the rest of the world that partnerships in international relations can be based on respect for different cultural traditions and religions.

In a global environment full of instability, unpredictability and shifting power balances nothing could be a more positive and hopeful sign for world peace.

Postscript:

so what are the prospects for Cyprus?

The EU has fulfilled all its promises, and Cyprus will now be admitted to membership of the Union in May 2004. The Cypriot people, at this moment – Greek Cypriot people alone – will be able to access all the benefits of membership. If intelligently and strategically harnessed, their established strengths should enable them further to develop Cyprus as a centre of excellence in a turbulent part of the world, in sectors such as finance, technology, intellectual property and the creative services.

For Cyprus this presents the opportunity to take the lead in the eastern Mediterranean and become the provider of choice for business-support services throughout this part of the world. The real value of this for Cypriot people lies in the scope for the enhanced prosperity and wealth accumulation it offers for the economy of the country, and the prospects for some greater measure of diversification from the country's heavy reliance on the tourist industry. For the EU, if Cyprus continues to develop its high-level business and commercial engagement, it presents the opportunity for extending Europe's influence into the Middle East and Arab nations.

And what of the parallel course? The UN peace process is now the focus of all attention. What is clear is that without the EU Kofi Annan would not have been in a position to have tabled his 150-page proposals for a solution in November 2002. Without the EU, Turkey would not have had the imperative to seek greater engagement from its Turkish Cypriot compatriots in the solution process. Without the EU, people in the north of Cyprus would not have felt the enormous sense of impending disadvantage that has driven them to demonstrate in their tens of thousands, calling for their leaders to engage with the EU and the UN plan or resign. Without the EU, the momentum and impetus for a solution would simply not have existed at this moment.

Whether or not the current drive ends in a solution depends on the continuing creativity of the international community, which is driving the process; the continuing courage of the Turkish Cypriot population in demanding its place in Europe alongside their Greek Cypriot partners; and the continuing good sense, calmness and political maturity of the Greek Cypriot people and their sometimes fickle party-political structures.

It is important to recognize the quite dramatic and refreshing changes which appear to be developing in Turkey. The new moderate Islamic Government is articulating a new approach and a new vision, which will serve its own European vocation well, and is hopefully helping to work towards a solution to the Cyprus problem. For the first time in recent history, Turkish leaders have largely abandoned the language of chauvinism and nationalism on the Cyprus problem, and on present performance appear to have adopted the European approach of dialogue and compromise. This must be very much welcomed and supported.

Cyprus has a bright and exciting future in the new Europe. However, its greatest prize can be achieved with reunification. Since the publication of the Kofi Annan plan there has been much discussion of its content and its pros and cons amongst all Cypriots. Naturally both sides have drawn up a schedule of issues which require further negotiation before it can be signed off – indeed they were asked to do so. The danger now is that the plan will run into the sand unless a process for progress can be secured that carries trust and integrity, and that has a clear set of principles underlying it.

This moment demands not just a juggling act between what can be considered possible by the two community leaders, Clerides and Denktash. Something more fundamental is at stake. Now the Annan plan is public property, and its conclusion has become not just a matter of political horse-trading, but crucially of gaining the trust and confidence of the people if the resultant solution is to be genuinely long-lasting, stable and just.

Boutros Boutros-Ghali referred to Europe as providing the only card on the table in 1995. That hand of cards has been played out, but not entirely to its conclusion. Europe could still offer the basic proposition for moving the process on. The closing stage of the negotiations on the Annan plan should take as its basic premise the underlying EU values of peaceful co-existence, dialogue, tolerance, respect of difference, solidarity, compromise and the defence and pursuit of individual rights, social justice and economic prosperity.

With Cyprus's route to the EU established and clearly carrying the support of the Turkish Cypriot people as well, the reality of a European vocation rather than the reality of a high-level political fix could succeed in giving the final text its public credibility and acceptability.

For instance, the text introduces some concepts like foreign appointees to the Supreme Court and the Board of the Central Bank. Some may argue that these provisions are sensible and pragmatic in the context of a newly united country where trust and confidence are at a premium. But the text does not allow for the nation state that is the newly united Cyprus to move beyond that point and, at some stage in its future, decide that it is ready to assume sole responsibility for its constitutional and financial life. In this respect, the pragmatic European approach of staged reviews, transitional periods and derogations could be an expedient to offer the prospect of European normality some time in the future.

Similarly, the security of the Turkish Cypriot people has always been one of the strongest demands of their negotiators. With Turkey now relaxing its opposition to the European Security and Defence Policy, and with the prospect of Turkey itself opening negotiations for membership of the EU shortly, Europe has become a focus for the security of all Cypriots, assuming that the Annan plan is adopted. Whilst the plan would see the Turkish army in the north of Cyprus diminish from its current level of 35,000, the three guarantor countries – the UK, Greece and Turkey – should be categoric about their future role. The plan allows for a monitoring committee of the guarantor powers. However, they need to confirm that they understand their responsibility and take it seriously by confirming just how they intend to manage the monitoring process.

Above all, these things are about establishing trust and confidence amongst the people. With the experience of the collapse of trust and confidence in Israel and Palestine, and the civil violence which still flares in Northern Ireland, it is clear that if we are to avoid such an outcome in Cyprus additional effort must be made to draw the people of Cyprus – both Greek Cypriot and Turkish Cypriot – into ownership of this plan. This is where the greatest effort is now needed.

Finally, it is of note that as we move towards the next round of discussions on the Annan plan, the wider European vision of peaceful co-existence and a shared vision for the region's future is beginning to find increasing adherents in the political elites of both Greece and Turkey. This can only serve both Greek and Turkish Cypriots well, and should encourage the development of European political values and vision in the political process and structures of the united Cyprus as well.

In terms of geostrategic politics, success has never offered such a glittering prize: Cyprus as a united country in the EU; Turkey on the road to entry; Turkey, Greece and Cyprus working together, and able to apply all the strengths of the EU in support of peace and stability in the eastern Mediterranean. Ultimately what is on offer is an eastern Mediterranean with an increasingly strong democratic basis, and an economy underpinned by the EU sensitized to the region through the accession of its new eastern Mediterranean members.

I firmly believe that a single international legal and constitutional entity is the only way forward for a united Cyprus. Such a federal government would be able to speak with authority on national issues, and is crucial for Cyprus's credibility and long-term national stability. There is also a very clear role for the two federated states to have a large measure of autonomy in local economic regeneration and the areas of policy that sit most closely to the people.

After 15 years of engagement with the cause of Cyprus, I sincerely believe that the coming challenges will be successfully overcome and a united Cyprus will take its place in the family of Europe.

January 2003

Index